Your book brilliantly explores the possibility that love, like art, might offer us that most exciting and creative thing: a transitional space. Love, your book suggests, assumes its own life, independent of its subjects. Your arguments are rigorous but your premises are cosmic.

— Chris Kraus

Delere Press
The Screaming Series

Écriture — Cri

Schreiben — Schrei

For, in every inscription — every writing by way of reading, writing that is reading — every scribere, there is always also the notion of tearing, ripping, perhaps even a mourning for what is unwritten, for the unwriteable in what is written ... written whilst tearing, with a small tear.

This paperback edition first published in 2016 by Delere Press LLP, as part of The Screaming Series.

First published in 2016 by
Delere Press LLP
www.delerepress.com
Delere Press LLP Reg No. T11LL1061K

ISBN 978-981-11-0532-6

Layout by Yanyun Chen

in fidelity

by Jeremy Fernando

pour K …

… an infinitesimal
abyss inhabits the
we that trembles
between us …

— Hélène Cixous

ON FIDELITY

I tell you yes.
I begin us
with a yes.
Yes begins us.

— Hélène Cixous

ON FIDELITY

And it is this « us » that is the site of thought. For, in order to begin thinking, we have to open a relationality between our selves and something, or someone; between our selves and another.

Thinking begins with a « yes ».

But, in order for that relationality to be opened, one would first have to be open to that, to its, possibility. Thus, it is an openness that precedes thinking, even as much as one is thinking as one opens that relationality: it is — and one might never quite be able to say with any certainty what 'it' is — both the condition and an approach to the possibility of thinking itself.

And here, we have to attend to the fact that it is not *one* who « begins us with a yes » but an « I ». So, not only is it an active decision, it is one that is made by a singular person — and in that moment of deciding, the « I » cannot escape, retreat, hide behind, universality: there is no duty, imperative, framework, that makes that decision for the « I ». It is only such as *I have chosen it* to be so. « I » have called « us » to begin with that « yes ». In fact, the decision to begin must have come before that « yes » — even as it can only come as the « yes » is uttered. Thus, opening oneself to a relationality with another resides in the « yes » : « yes » is the very condition and juncture of relationality that we are speaking of.

But, if opened by an « I », then perhaps it is only that of Hélène Cixous. And by reading her « I », do I then also make it mine, make her mine? Which opens the question of its legitimacy: for my reading of her « I » may never have had anything to do with her: the « I » might well only be voices in my head. Which might suggest that one has moved back into the realm of an imperative, a duty, a call: but where one can never quite be certain from where this call is emanating, where it is coming from. So, perhaps the risk here is not just that by responding to a call one might be making it one's own, but that acknowledging the possibility that it might be a call already opens the possibility of « us » ; an « us » that could only happen because of the intervention of the « I ». The answering that might have already happened when one says « yes » to the possibility of the call, to the possibility that it is a call.

An openness, an opening, that resides in a « yes », *even as yes, it, is only opened by an I.* A « yes » that is preceded by a yes-ness of the yes; *a yes-ness that can only be called into being by an I who cannot yet know of it.* Or, perhaps even a « yes » that always carries with it a yes-ness that escapes the yes.

For, even as the « yes » is opened, this is an affirmation that cannot be a complete affirmation: if that were so, this would be a « yes » that completely consumes the object that it is purporting to open a relationality with — at that point, the object or person that the « I » is in a relationality with is subsumed under the self; which would be the end of the possibility of that relationality. Perhaps here, it is the notion of *possibility* that we have to pay most attention to; keeping in mind that potentiality is not merely a phase preceding actuality. Which is not to say that nothing will happen; not only can we not quite be sure of that, if it were so, it would no longer be a potentiality. Nor it is — as Giorgio Agamben likes to say — a « potential-to-be and a potential-not-to-be ». For, if that were so, the « not-to-be » would lie beyond potentiality. Whilst there is something that quite possibly escapes potentiality, this is a beyond that is not outside the realm of potentiality, but within it. Thus, true potentiality is the *potential-to-be* and an *impotentiality not-to-be*, a potentiality that negates itself as a negation, but still shimmers there, as a possibility of a non-negation.[1]

In other words, even as there is a « yes», in order for it to be an opening to thinking, to thought, it has to always also carry the spectre of a « no » in it. And if thought is an openness to possibility — otherwise it would merely be a moment before action, be a precursor to doing — there then has to be the potential for thought to not only amount to nothing, but also be non-thought itself. But this would not be a non-thought that is an antonym to thinking, a negation of thought, but a thinking that thinks itself as non-thinking, or a non-thinking that is already thinking; a « no » within a « yes » ; a no that quite possibly carries echoes of yes-ness within it; the two perhaps remaining indistinguishable.

A « yes » carrying echoes of a « no ».

A « yes » that opens the possibility of a relationality, a possibility that is maintained as such only by the possibility of a « no » within; a « no » that perhaps cuts, but that never quite wounds. A cut that opens: keeping in mind Jean-Luc Nancy's reminder that « it is space that is needed for touch to begin in the first place ».[2] Perhaps then, a « no » that not only maintains the proper distance between the two saying « yes », the two that attempt to open a relationality with each other, but more than that, the « no » that opens the possibility for « yes » to even « begin us ».

***

A « no » that we find in the opening line of Hanif Kureishi's novel *Intimacy* — « It is the saddest night, for I am leaving and not coming back »[3] — a « no » uttered by the protagonist, Jay, to no one in particular, perhaps not even himself. For, one must try to remember that even as one encounters his thoughts at the beginning, that even as they touch one at the start, Jay spends most of the novel doing absolutely nothing. And more than that, it is this « no » that opens his reflection on, his recounting of, of his relationship with his wife, Susan, his two children; meditating upon them in a way that it seems that he has never before done. So, even as he is ostensibly enacting, or at least uttering, a cut, a break, from them, he is also opening another — perhaps even more intimate — relationship with them.

And in this way, the time he remains with them — eventually he does leave — is « a time that pulses and moves within chronological time, that transforms chronological time from within ».[4] Whilst it may seem strange to evoke Agamben's meditation of messianic time here, one should not forget that the realm of memory, of remembering, is not just achronological, ahistorical, nor merely historical, chronological; it is a time that evokes what has already happened, and whilst doing so always also brings what is recalled back to one in the present. However, this particular *parousia* involves a second coming of an event that may or may not have happened. And here, one should never forget that one has no control over forgetting. Thus, not only is each memory potentially unreliable, one can never quite be sure if each act of memory, remembering, might always already have forgetting written into it. Where even if what one remembers is true, has a truth, *aletheia*, there might always be a certain forgetting, oblivion, *lethe*, inscribed in it.[5] Perhaps, here, one might even open the register that forgetting is the very condition of memory itself: for, if there is no forgetting, there would never be any need to remember in the first place. Thus, when one remembers, one is not only recalling a time that has past, one is also potentially calling forth a possibility that has not quite happened, a future-possibility; not from somewhere outside one's own time, but from the time that remains within one's own past, one's own time. Which — reopening our registers to Agamben — « can only mean a radical transformation of our experience of time»,[6] or, if one prefers, times.

Moreover, we should recall Agamben's lesson that « the messianic is not the end of time but the time of the end. What is messianic is not the end of time but the relation of every moment, every *kairos*, to the end of time, and to eternity ».[7] Which suggests that — without even needing a divine notion to time here — it is a time which always already knows its own end, without actually knowing where the end is; a time which bears in mind a time when it is no longer time; a time which has non-time in time.

Thus, time in relation with its other.

And what else is a relationality other than an attempt to be in relation with another;[8] a relationality that calls to another and yet never subsumes the other under its self; in Alain Badiou's conception, a « construction, a life that is being made, no longer from the perspective of the One but from the perspective of Two ».[9] As Badiou would call it, the moment of Love: keeping in mind that « love always starts with an encounter. And I would give this encounter the quasi-metaphysical status of an *event*, namely of something that doesn't enter into the immediate order of things ».[10] This is not a fusing of two into one, the romantic notion that continues to haunt thinking of love, a notion that not only — as in classic mythology — leads towards death, but more importantly, leads to the effacement of one by another, an effacement of relationality itself. Instead, this is love that « invents a new way of lasting in life … a new way of experiencing time ».[11] Where the invention involves the transformation of the « absolute contingency of [an] encounter with someone I didn't know [into something that] finally takes on the appearance of destiny ».[12]

In other words, love as the moment in which another time is written into one's; the time of an other that transforms one's time whilst always also remaining other, always also remaining a time that remains.

A time with, a time in tune with another time yet not reduced to, nor reducing it to, the same time: with time; contemporaneous. With and not-with at the same time. An impossible time. And, it is this impossibility that Hanif Kureishi explores in *Intimacy*; in which Jay is contemplating leaving his wife Susan, in the hopes of rekindling a storied affair with Nina. But what is holding him back is the possibility of losing contact with his two children. Thus, it is a case of three different intimacies coming together in and through the narrative. And since each of these intimacies is explored through Jay, through a first person narrative, these are relationalities that are recalled, remembered; in their own time whilst within time, through Jay, through the one in the time, in the times, of the two.

And it is precisely the protagonist's indecision that saves him from falling into the banal new age notion of 'fulfilling oneself'; where one is supposed to live out one's dreams and desires. For, all his different intimacies are pulling at him to choose them. Where even as he is leaving Susan, memories of their life together continually haunt him; at the same time, he cannot bear to leave his children; all whilst the memory of his time with Nina is drawing him towards her, even as he no longer knows where she is. To compound matters, since one only hears of them through Jay, one can never be sure if they are merely voices in his head. In this way, his indecision is not merely a refusal to decide, it is also an attempt — maybe a futile one — to respond to all the different intimacies; an irresponsibility perhaps, but one should bear in mind that Jay is also failing to respond to himself, his self. In this way, the tale is attempting to think the possibility that caring for another often entails the effacement of one's own self. Hence, the importance of lying: « lying protects us all; it keeps the importance going. It is a kindness to lie … A world without lying would be impossible; a world in which lying wasn't deprecated is also impossible ».[13] Which suggests that it isn't easy to lie. It is in some way the greatest gift to another. For, lying « creates a terrible loneliness » ; one is the only one who knows what happened. This isn't a lying that hides oneself, protects oneself: this is a lying that exposes one to no other than oneself; a lying that cuts one from another, quite possible from the time of another, from the time that is the other.

In order to protect the possibility of intimacy.

For, if *two become one* entails being exactly the same as another, it would be the very definition of narcissism. Thus, the danger lies in attempting to make a figure of speech literal. And this, Kureishi locates in the troubled marriage: through their love for their children, their lives have collapsed into each other's to the point where they no longer are singular persons, but a couple, a single entity. For, one must never forget, that even as one needs, we need, closeness for intimacy, *two become one* must remain metaphorical, a metaphor; where there can be a movement, a carrying (*pherein*) across (*meta*). For, if we allow ourselves to momentarily recall Nancy's reminder, in order to touch someone, space — in-between — is first needed.[14]

***

Here perhaps, it might be the time to attempt to open the dossier of fidelity; and, in particular, attend to the question of the relationality between fidelity and its object, to the question of *must there be an object to fidelity?*. For, if one is faithful to something or someone, is one responding to the *what*, the characteristics of the thing, the person, or the *who*, the person, thing, as such? Which is not to say that *what* and *who* are necessarily distinguishable, separable, to begin with. However, if we open the register that the *who* is always already beyond us — outside of knowability, even if only slightly — this opens the possibility that it is the spectre, the potentially unknowable, that haunts all relationality. Thus, even if there is an object to one's fidelity — for, without which one cannot even begin to speak of fidelity, speak of relationality — this might well be an *objectless object* or, at least, an object that remains veiled from one.

And whenever we open the dossier of *fidelity*, the notion of *love* is, of course, quite possibly, never far behind. A notion that one often encounters through — a notion that might well come through, call to us through — the phrase *I love you*. A phrase that Badiou reminds us « is usually thought to be completely meaningless and banal [but, what it also says — and here I am, perhaps irresponsibly, disregarding one's intentions, or even the subject who utters the sentence — is], I shall extract something else from what was mere chance. I'm going to extract something that will endure, something that will persist, a commitment, a fidelity ».[15] When one says to another *I love you*, « you say that to someone living, standing there in front of you, but you are also addressing something that cannot be reduced to this simple material presence, something that is absolutely and simultaneously both beyond and within ».[16] Or, perhaps even, something that is absolutely simultaneously beyond whilst — extracted — within. And even as one posits that one « extract[s] something that will endure », the thing that lasts, that stays with the two, that might well be the sign of fidelity, is perhaps only to come, *avenir, peut-être même à venir*. Thus, *I love you*, is an utterance of relation, of a relationality between an « I » and a « you » ; a relationality — particularly if the other, both others, remain wholly other — in which the two in relation with each other remain unknowns, where the other remains veiled. And, if love is the openness of one to another, it is a relationality where the « I » is altered, perhaps in ways that one remains blind to. More than that, since the two — the « I » and the « you » — are, remain, unknown, the relationality itself — love itself — might well also remain hidden from one.

Thus, *I love you* is an utterance of relationality that does nothing more, or less, than promises relationality between one and the other — an utterance in fidelity to the possibility of a relationality.

And here, as the dossier of promises is opened, one might hear echoes of Werner Hamacher's teaching: that « whenever there is a promise, something other than the promise and something other than language — or simply another language — is also spoken. What is promised is always something other than understanding, other than another understanding, and other than an alteration of understanding alone. Something unpromisable ».[17] Something that is always already not of the promise; not in the sense of being excluded from promises, certainly not antonymous to promises, but something that escapes being promised even as it is part of the promise. For, in order to promise, there has to be something that is only to come, something not quite yet, something beyond; where the something that is promised cannot even have the status of a thing, or at least a known thing — therefore, there can never be a referent to the promise. Which means that even as it is being promised — keeping in mind that promises can only take place as a relation, in relation to another — it is a relationality where the promisory utterance, statement — without which there cannot be any promise — is one that is without correspondence, is *catachrestic*. A statement, an utterance, that not only cannot be verified, but might never be verifiable. But, which might well have occurred without one ever even knowing — a coming to be outside of, exterior to, what one knows, one thinks, one has uttered. Which means that it is not so much whether it is promised or not, but that the « unpromisable » cannot be promised because one can not know of it even when one has uttered it. Or, even: the « unpromisable » cannot be promised precisely because even when it is uttered, it is not, cannot be, is not quite yet, stated.

Thus, « promising means nothing else — a promise of the mere possibility of making promises ». Which is not to say that the one that is promising is not responsible for the promise, for the utterance of the promise; for, one must never forget that even as it is perhaps always only in potentiality, it must also be uttered. A promise only exists — if it can be said to exist, to be; but, at least, it is always in becoming — in and through language. Keeping in mind that oftentimes language says far more, or far less, something other, than what we are saying, writing. Or, to turn to Hamacher once again: « speaking a language means nothing else than speaking as one who does not yet have a language »[19] — as one who is speaking as if one can speak a language — as one who is doing nothing other than promising to speak a language.

Speaking in fidelity to the possibility of speaking a language; perhaps, especially when one is attempting to speak of fidelity, in fidelity, to another.

Perhaps especially when one is uttering *I love you.*

Which opens the possibility that not only does the « I » never quite know what (s)he, one, it, is uttering — that one is uttering in blind faith to the possibility of love, in the hope of a fidelity to come —but that at the point of love, the « I » and the « you » might well be in a relationality that brings with it the possibility of a non-relation.

A relationality that puts the two in relation with each other, whilst at the same time maintains a distance within that relationality itself.

A relationality that perhaps even utters — allowing for a moment an utterance that comes from a relationality rather than from the subjects in relation with; an utterance that springs forth from the *with* — a relationality that might even mutter, stutter …

… « I would prefer not to ».

***

A response — Bartleby's response — that foregrounds the fact that it is the « I » that « prefers not to » : not that *I cannot* nor *I will not* but that this is a preference. That it is not based on anything other than a decision by the « I » : when asked

« *why* do you refuse » by Mr B, his boss, Bartleby's response is simply, « I would prefer not to ».[20] Thus, to read this response, Bartleby's response, as an absolute refusal would be untrue: just because he « prefers not to » does not mean that he will not.[21] But just because it is not a complete rejection of the request also does not mean that it is a delayed compliance: Mr B comes to realise, rather quickly, that « his decision was irreversible ».[22]

So, even as it an inclination — and like all preferences, one that might well be unjustifiable — its effects, in relation with every situation, every moment in which there is a response, are lasting.

Quite a few thinkers — Agamben and Slavoj Žižek amongst them — have attempted to read Bartleby's response as a form of passive resistance. Their claim is that his response, that is always also a non-response, short-circuits the system. That if he had out-rightly rejected his boss there would have been an immediate expulsion, firing: for, in Mr B's words, « had there been the least uneasiness, anger, impatience or impertinence in his manner; in other words, had there been anything ordinarily human about him, doubtless I should have violently dismissed him from the premises ».[23] The trouble was, as Mr B continues, « there was something about Bartleby that not only strangely disarmed me, but in a wonderful manner, touched and disconcerted me ».[24] And here, Mr B makes what one might call the fatal error: « I began to reason with him ».[25]

Whilst most readings, readers, focus on Bartleby, perhaps we could momentarily turn our attention to the other interlocutors, those that are attempting to elicit not just a response but a particular act, action, from him. I — allowing all echoes of the unjustifiability of my choice — would like to propose that they were unable to move him, influence his actions, have power over him, if you prefer, as they had structured their statements as requests. By doing so, not only did they open the possibility of non-compliance, they had made a far more fundamental mistake: requests function on the logic that both parties involved are operating under the same rules, form, customs, reason — in other words, the exchange is one that involves pre-set options, and not actual choices. That in a situation, to echo Mr B, « a slight hint would suffice — in short, an assumption ».[26] The assumption being that the one receiving the address would know what to do, even the right thing to do, that one is adroit — allowing all echoes of the law, *droit*, to resound — at knowing what to do.

Perhaps what is truly subversive about Bartleby's response is that it takes Mr B's questions seriously, takes it as a question which offers the potential for a true response. And by doing so, Bartleby challenges authority to reveal itself — to not hide behind the illusion that it is offering a choice. That even as Mr B thinks otherwise, authority is no more than « vulgar bullying ».[27] In other words, what Bartleby does is to challenge daddy to show himself.

Here, we might tune our registers to the dossier that Avital Ronell opens in *Loser Sons*, where she teaches us that authority is hinged around the figure of the *auctor*, the origin, the father.[28] It is crucial to note that authority rests in, revolves around, the figure — more than the person, the body — of the father: which means that the one in authority must live up to the idea of authority; it is not so much who one is, or even what one does, as long as one's actions, and one, is perceived to be authoritative, have authority. This plays out most significantly at moments when one's authority is seen to be tested: for, if daddy has to impose the whip, (s)he no longer has any authority; it is only truly authoritative when one does not have to use any force. In other words, authority triumphs when one is doing what daddy expects — without her having to say, let alone do, anything. Authority is based on no more than a hint, an assumption. Authority responds to the test not just by subsuming the tester under its figure — by hinting at what the one testing should do — but more importantly by showing the tester that it is precisely daddy that allows this very test to happen in the first place. Thus, the one who is authoring the authority is not so much daddy but the one under her authority — one writes, authors, authorises, one's own subjugation. And, one finds Mr B coming to grasp with the true radicality of Bartleby's response in his summation of his scrivener's replies: « you are decided then, not to comply with my request — a request made according to common usage and common sense ».[29] Bartleby's challenge lies in his refusal to accept a prescribed notion of « common » ; his insistence that even though he is a scrivener, he can inscribe his version, or at least open a negotiation of what is common in any particular situation. To compound matters, it was not as if Bartleby could be threatened, coaxed, or even bribed to alter his position: which might be what is truly terrifying about his response.[30]

And here, one might recall why, of the totalitarian regimes, the Khmer Rouge were particularly terrifying: it was not as if there were no other regimes that were fond of killing their own people; it was the fact that they were utterly incorruptible, that they could not be persuaded of another possibility, other possibilities, that they were so rational they were beyond common sense, beyond reason itself. This can be seen in *Le portail*, François Bizot's haunting account of the early days of the Khmer Rouge. Much of the text hinges on Bizot's uneasy friendship with his captor Douch, developed over the three months he spent as the latter's prisoner. Far from being a brutal captor, Douch is portrayed as a principled idealist, beyond corruption, and totally committed to the cause. But it is not as if the Douch that is better known — the Douch that is head of the infamous S-21 torture centre, Tuol Sleng — cannot be detected as well. In that sense, it is not a descent into brutality, a fall of the man in spite of his ideals, the idea, but that the murderous rampage is part of the ideology itself. And nowhere, at no point, is this better captured than in Douch's own words: « It's better to have a sparsely populated Cambodia than a country full of incompetents! »[31]

Perhaps one can also contend that Bartleby's insistence on his position — even to his own detriment — demonstrates an inability to learn: he ends up in jail, and eventually is assumed to have died alone and penniless, or at least to have drifted away, forgotten by everyone, except perhaps Mr B. In this sense, Bartleby is the figure of the idiot *par excellence*. And it is the radical stupidity of the idiot — the refusal, or perhaps inability, to see, learn, be infected by, the symbolic structure of language — that always keeps it (for gendering the idiot would already bring it, tame it, under language) before language, pre-language, *infans*. And, if we retune our receptors to Ronell, she teaches us that « stupidity has to do with our nature as finite beings; it is the limit of the limit — the limited — a mark of our temporal condition in and as lapse. Yet it is not itself limited, touching even infinity … »[32] Thus, even as one is limited, finite, it is precisely stupidity that opens the possibility of going beyond knowing, beyond cognition, beyond our self, even as this going beyond might always already be a step not-beyond.

But perhaps, this step — a step that must have happened otherwise it would not be a step — that is both beyond and not-beyond at the same time is a step that marks the point, the border, the frame. Keeping in mind that a frame collects, keeps within, brings into itself, whilst, at the very same time, leaves out, keeps out, excludes. Not that these are antonymous: for, by its very inclusion, gathering, bringing together, it ejects, removes, pushes away. To compound matters, one should also not forget that to frame is to accuse someone of something that the person might not have done: which opens the possibility that the exclusion could well be based on a bias, a slant. However, without said slant there is also no possibility of perspective, thinking, thought. For, as Umberto Eco posits — once again reopening the register of stupidity — discernment, choice, saying no, is a mark of intelligence: « discriminating what you want to learn and remember is critical from a cognitive standpoint … If culture did not filter, it would be inane — as inane as the formless, boundless Internet is on its own. And if we all possessed the boundless knowledge of the Web, we would be idiots! »[33] Which might well be — if I allow myself a little detour here — an echo, even perhaps a transcription, of Heraclitus' testimony from a few years earlier: that « not far form the ancient city of Miletus lived the son of Teutamas, whose name was Bias. I would have known, this one man more than others earned the good esteem of worthy people ». (Fragment 112)[34] Allowing also for the irony that there might well be a bias in choosing, declaring, Bias as an exemplar of good esteem — just as there might well be a slant in selecting, enframing, any example, any citation, any source, one marshals for one's thought.

And here, one should try not to forget that in selecting, choosing, any particular instance, example, source, one is always also enacting, performing, a violence onto it; even as one might be paying homage, attempting to respond, to it. For, there is always a certain affinity with a text, a source, before one cites it — whether the relationality is one of like or dislike is perhaps irrelevant here. So, even as one attempts to be as fair, as responsible, to the text, every citation is always already a wrenching out of context, a reframing in another context; more specifically, one's own context. In other words — and here, it might be responsible to foreground that one is using, in perhaps the harshest sense of *making use of*, *exploiting*, the words of another — one might well be making the other say, accusing the other of saying, what they might never have; framing the other as one is enframing them.

Thus, even as one frames, the frame itself marks the « limit of the limit ». So, even as one says something that might be recognisable, be recognised, is within what might be cognisable, knowable, perhaps even construed as knowledge, it is perhaps only made possible by not just what is outside itself, beyond itself, but also by its own limitless limit.

Perhaps even its own stupidity.

***

... her name is Dulcinea, her country El Toboso, a village of La Mancha, her rank must be at least that of a princess, since she is my queen and mistress, for in her are realised all the impossible and chimerical attributes of beauty that poets assign to ladies; for her hair is gold; her forehead Elysian fields; her eyebrows rainbows; her eyes suns; her cheeks roses; her lips coral; her teeth pearls; her neck alabaster; her bosom marble; her hands ivory; her fairness snow; and those parts that modesty has concealed from human sight are such, I think and trust, that discretion can praise them, but make no comparison.

Why do fools fall in love? Why do birds sing so gay? And lovers await the break of day Why do they fall in love?

— Frankie Lymon & Morris Levy

The fool, the clown, the *picaro* — for, whenever one hears of love, especially a love that is intensely devout, that occurs, perhaps even survives, in spite of all circumstances, situations, particularities, it is not too difficult to hear the voice of Don Quixote, calling out, declaring his service, dedicating his life even, to Lady Dulcinea, or more aptly, his Lady Dulcinea. Despite the fact that — or, to be fair once again, according to Sancho Panza — « ... I can tell you that she can pitch the iron bar as well as the strongest lad in the whole village. God save us! She's a lusty lass, tall and straight, with hair on her chest, who can pull the chestnuts out of the fire for any knight errant now or to come who has her for his lady ».[35] It would be too easy to say that infatuation has pulled the wool over the Don's eyes, and that he cannot see her for who and what she really is. That, in spite of everyone — even his trusty squire — pointing out that Dulcinea is really Aldonzo Lorenzo, the Knight of the Rueful Figure sees her as the fairest lady in the world.[36]

However, one should not forget that his madness — the catalyst, as it were, of his transfiguration from Quixana to a knight — comes from, through, too many books on chivalry, from too much reading. In this sense, one can — echoing the register of Avital Ronell's wonderful reading of *Madame Bovary* in *Crack Wars*, where she teases out the possibility that Emma's addictions to pharmaceuticals and reading are not necessarily completely distinguishable[37] — open the dossier that it is not so much that Quixana is seeing things that are not there, that he is in a flight of fancy as it were, but that he is seeing new possibilities in what is in front of him, in reality itself. This distinction between fancy and possibilities — or between fancy and imagination as Wallace Stevens would put it — lies in one's relationship with reality itself. Fancy, as Stevens posits in *The Necessary Angel* is an attempt to break with, separate from, reality; imagination is an attempt to be in the world, but not in a way that is bound by convention, repetition, habits, mores, culture even.[37] In other words, imagination is a throwing of oneself into the world, where one's *habitus* is not merely habit, merely habitual; an attempt to respond to the world in such a way that there is a momentary cut — not from the world, but in the world itself. Thus, imagination is a manner of opening oneself to the possibility of a relationality; one that is not quite there yet, where the relation itself has not yet formed, but where one acts as if it has already done so.

Poetry is not about seeing the invisible, or the very visible. Poetry, instead, is about seeing the slightly visible.

— Michel Deguy

Which might be why, to everyone else, the one who imagines might seem to be mad, to be out of her mind, to be quite literally seeing things. Or, more aptly, seeing things that no one else can see — not because they are not there, not because they are not looking hard enough, but perhaps because they are not looking blindly. For, if knowledge, if knowing, is based on correspondence, it is always also in the realm of memory — what is known is also what one recalls, calls back to oneself. Thus, it is a relationality between one, a subject, and the object one remembers. However, since forgetting happens to one — one can neither control when it strikes us, nor what one forgets — this suggests that there is no necessary object to forgetting; or, at least, no object that can be known to the one who forgets. Hence, one might never be able to detect if one has forgotten, even retrospectively. And more than that, since forgetting can come and go as it pleases, since it is beyond the possibility of knowing, it remains but a name referring to nothing except the fact that it is a name, a catachrestic metaphor that moves in and out, quite possibly independently of one's cognition. Thus, there is no reason to believe that each act of memory might not have forgetting inscribed in it. Which opens the possibility that this moment of madness, this moment of seeing what no one else sees, is also a glimpse into forgetting. Not that one can articulate it — for, the moment it is uttered, one is back into an attempted correspondence, into memory. But, at the same time, one almost always articulates it, if only to express the fact that one does not, cannot, know what one has forgotten — through the enigmatic utterance, the utterance of an enigma, *I forgot.*[39] Thus, an utterance of a memory — since it can be, and is, uttered — but a memory that is not shared by anyone else, not even one self. And what one's utterance, this utterance, makes all too clear is that it is often quite impossible to distinguish with any certainty between fancy and imagination: for, if one cannot know if one's recollection has any correspondence with the world, with what has happened, one cannot know if it has anything to do with reality. Thus, at that moment of seeing, of bringing back before oneself, one is always seeing blindly; in the precise sense of there being an inherent blindness in one's sight, not just because there is something one might have missed out, or that one might have seen something that others cannot, not just because one can never be sure if what one is seeing is actually there — that there is an unknowability in all referentiality — but that one must make a leap of faith that one is actually seeing, that one can even see, that there is a possibility of knowing, that one can even know.

And perhaps seeing what is not seen by others is not so much seeing what they cannot see, but an acknowledgment — foregrounding even — that even as one is seeing, one is always already seeing blindly.

Where blindness is both the limit, and the necessary condition, of seeing itself.

Which might be why he is the Rueful Knight: for, what he is sorrowful about is the fact that not only can no one else see the Lady Dulcinea that is in Aldonzo Lorenzo, but that even as he can name her as the fairest of ladies, her beauty is « impossible and chimerical », a beauty that is only that which « poets assign to ladies » — a beauty that is such perhaps only because he has named her « my queen and mistress ». Or, even: that her beauty is « impossible » as it is only in his naming her as « queen and mistress » ; and that it will — Dulcinea will — always remains « chimerical », even to him.

Which brings us back to the beginning, to the question of the relationality between love and the *who* and the *what* — to that of: do we love someone for *who* they are, or *what* they are. And, even as they remain potentially inseparable, one perhaps catches a glimpse of the *who* in these moments of foolishness, in these moments when everyone else calls one mad, a fool. Not that one might necessarily be able to know what this glimpse even is; but only that one names it so: in the moment that one names the other as the loved one — in the moment of uttering *I love you*.

Perhaps then, not so much *why do fools fall in love*, but that one has to be a fool to fall in love.

Where the risk is precisely that of *falling* itself. Not just when love fails, but perhaps even more so when there is a momentary opening of the Two between one and another. Where, in that moment, there is a coming together — even as both remain wholly other from each other. And here, one should never forget the risks involved in any potential communion: for, as Georges Bataille teaches us: « communication cannot proceed from one full and intact individual to another. It requires individuals whose separate existence in themselves is *risked*, placed at the limit of death and nothingness; the moral summit is the moment of risk taking, it is a being suspended in the beyond of oneself, at the limit of nothingness ... »[40] Perhaps then, the risk is precisely that the two can no longer quite remain wholly other, cannot remain whole: that what is opened, ruptured even, is quite possibly the self.

That at that point, he is really no longer Alonso Quixana but is Don Quixote.

As to *why do they fall in love?*, if the question is one that is calling for a reasonable response, a response of reason, perhaps the only possible reply is another question: *why do birds sing so gay?*

Which is perhaps a way of saying: *I don't know.*

But, it is perhaps this unknowing, this potential unknowability, that reopens the possibilities once again. For, if one does not know, there is then also the possibility that not only might one find out, but that one might always also be imagining one's responses. Almost as if one is — at least momentarily — not bound by limits, by mores, boundaries, by language itself. Almost as if one is, for a brief moment, before language, pre-language — a child.

Infans.

***

Where, the figure of the *infans* invites us to reopen the dossier — or in the spirit of things, the register I am foregrounding, that I would prefer to foreground is — of Bartleby's response, in particular, the possibility of him *making his own choice.* An imaginative response: one that refuses the boundaries that the other assumes one would draw for oneself. That takes the possibility of language itself seriously, and by doing so echoes Nietzsche's reminder that each act of writing (*schreiben*) quite possibly brings with it a scream (*schreien*); one that tears open, apart, punctures, perhaps even undoes precisely what is written, inscribed, ascribed, let alone prescribed.

The *scream of the scrivener*

… as it were.

Where, the effect of Bartleby's response is not just on the possibility of his own imagination, but also on the imagination of his boss: he becomes an « intolerable incubus »[41] to Mr B. We see this most obviously in the incident where Mr B, at his wits end since Bartleby refuses to budge, decides to move. However, even after he has done so, Bartleby continues to be a spectre in his life — letters are sent to Mr B's new office requesting, almost demanding, that he does something about the one who « persists in haunting the building generally, sitting upon the banisters of the stairs by day, and sleeping in the entry by night ».[42] Almost a perfect manifestation of the Indignatos slogan in Spain: *if you do not let us dream, we will not let you sleep*. Where what has been occupied is not an office space — that would be too banal — but the imagination of Mr B himself. Where he even begins to hear Bartleby in everything, even when people are not talking about his scrivener.[43]

si no nos dejáis soñar, no os dejaremos dormer

Here, we can finally fully appreciate the futility in Mr B's lament: « since he will not quit me, I must quit him ».[44] For, even though there was an overt attempt to shift location — move into a new context to be out of contact, as it were — he always already knew that it would not have worked: he had long inscribed Bartleby into his being.

So, it is not just that in his statement « I would prefer not to», Bartleby is, as Agamben and Žižek suggest, being transgressive by becoming *anything you want me to be* but, more radically, he has infected Mr B's imagination by being *in anything*, in everything. And, it is not so much that Bartleby transfigures himself to fit in with the desires of Mr B, but that — by being such an enigma — he has seduced his boss into attempting to « reason with him » ; and thus, input logic onto him, write onto him.

> Authoring Bartleby such that he becomes his *significant other*, keeping in mind that this is not of the order of meaning — it is not a relationship of signification, but significance.

If one wanted to, at this juncture, one could channel the spectres of Gilles Deleuze and Felix Guattari, and call it a relationality with a strong field of intensity. Whilst this might appear to be a throwaway comment — an opening of a dossier for no good reason — we should remember that not only might we be attempting to tread into a zone where reason has long left the building, but that it is precisely in these zones — these moments of seeming divergences, such as when he is walking along the street and overhears a conversation that has naught to do with his scrivener — that Mr B's thoughts go foremost to Bartleby. Here, we should recall the scene just before Mr B moves from his office: at the point where he is grappling with « resentment » towards Bartleby, he is stopped by the recollection of the « divine injunction: 'A new commandment give I unto you; that ye love one another' ».[45] A love in the precise sense of opening himself to the possibility that is Bartleby, to the point of « construing his conduct. Poor fellow, poor fellow! thought I, he don't mean anything; and besides, he has seen hard times, and ought to be indulged ».[46] Where Mr B starts writing a Bartleby in order to justify his own acts, perhaps his own beliefs, even as much as we will never has access to that — or, perhaps even to save reason itself.

Authoring Bartleby — authorising Bartleby.

Where, one could read *Bartleby the Scrivener: A Story of Wall Street* as a tale of resistance, a tale of how a singular response — in terms of each response happening in a particular moment, time, place, but also the uniqueness of both Bartleby and his reply — ruptures the structure of authority, reverses it even as it is irreversible, seduces the other to reverse itself precisely due to its irreversibility. But that would be a slightly limited reading. For, what would be left out is another possibility: that it is also a story of love. For, one should try to never forget that authority requires relationality, that relationality is the very condition of authority — one must still author the other before authority is enacted on oneself. Thus, always also a tale of opening to the possibility of another, of being infected by another, of being inscribed by and inscribing another onto oneself; opened by Mr B's very first « yes » — from that moment henceforth, opening himself to Bartleby.

Not a « yes » that is of the order of reason — how was Mr B ever to know — nor a « yes » that is calculated. But a « yes » that — bringing with it echoes of Hélène Cixous — whispers ...

I love you:

I work at understanding you

to the point of not understanding you, and there, standing in a wind, I don't understand you. Not understanding in a way of holding myself in front and of letting come. Transverbal, transintellectual relationship, this loving the other in submission to the mystery. (It's accepting, not knowing, forefeeling, feeling with the heart.) I'm speaking in favour of non-recognition, not of mistaken cognition. I'm speaking of closeness, without any familiarity.[47]

Which is why *I love you* is never two-way: for, just because it is an utterance that opens to the possibility of a relationality does not mean that it is reciprocal. And, even if it is reciprocated, it is a reciprocity that is another *I love you* — another one-way; and, perhaps more importantly, another utterance that is made in the same blindness as the first.

Another utterance that might have naught to do with the other.

For, as Roland Barthes shows us, « proffering cannot be double (doubled): only the *single flash* will do, in which two forces join (separate, divided, they would not exceed some ordinary agreement). For the *single flash* achieves this unheard-of thing: the abolition of responsibility. Exchange, gift, and theft (the only known forms of economy) each in its way implies heterogeneous objects and a dislocated time: my desire against something else — and this always requires the time for drawing up the agreement. Simultaneous proffering establishes a movement whose model is socially unknown, unthinkable: neither exchange, nor gift, nor theft, our proffering, welling up in crossed fires, designates an expenditure which relapses nowhere and whose very community abolishes any thought of reservation: we enter each by means of the other into absolute materialism ».[48] And, not just materialism in the sense of conditions, contexts, particularities, situations; but also, and perhaps more importantly, in the unknowability of the object, in the unknowability that the other, both others, plunge themselves into as they become objects.

Which is why « I hallucinate what is *empirically* impossible: that our two profferings be made *at the same time* ». But,

... time is a tease. Time is a tease because everything has to happen in its own time.

— André Breton

perhaps possible if one considers the possibility that love is the opening of the time of the two, of two in their own time. A dream perhaps, a hallucination even. After all, it would not quite be a dream if it were already possible. However, in order to dream of something, to imagine it, it would also have to be within one's realm of possibility — at the very least, one would have to be able to conceive of it. Perhaps then, the dream of simultaneity is an impossible possibility: possible only if we take seriously the impossibility of the simultaneous.

Perhaps then, only in a time which « cannot designate a chronological period or duration but, instead, must represent nothing less than a qualitative change in how time is experienced ».[50] Which suggests that it is not time itself that is altered — how could that even be — but one's relationship to it. Thus, a relationality that might never be able to be felt by anyone but oneself; or even, it might well be a relationality to oneself that is at stake here. After all, one should recall again that this is a time that Giorgio Agamben calls, the « time of the messiah »,[51] messianic time. One that is « not the end of time, but the time of the end » — where « to experience the 'time of the end,' can only mean a radical transformation of our experience of time ».[52] Keeping in mind that this is a « time that pulses and moves within chronological time, that transforms chronological time from within ».[53] Not that chronology is altered, but the manner in which one experiences it: for what is radically transformed, is changed at the root, is oneself. For, one should not, even as one tends to, forget that the « I » is always already plural; even grammatically. (S)he loves — I love. Perhaps always already an indication, a reminder, of its own otherness — perhaps even to itself.

Thus, it is a situation where one is both in time and in another time, at the same time: where one is contemporary. Perhaps then, keeping in mind that *I love you* is an attempt to open a relationality; it is an opening, an utterance, that « distends time, an *already* that is also a *not yet*, a delay that does not put off until later but, instead, a disconnection within the present moment that allows us to grasp time ».[54] For, without this momentary delay, this disconnection, there would not be the gap, the space-between, for the other *I love you*; for the response from another, to be an actual response. Where, it is a relationality, an opening to the event, to the possibility of the Two, only in the moment when the *I love you* doesn't merely assume an automatic affirmation, isn't seeking a banal reaction — where it opens itself to the possibility of a rejection, even a non-response — but at the same time remains open to a possible response that is to come. In fact, is uttered *as if* the response is to come — never expectantly, but always already in hope.

Perhaps only awaiting.

Bearing in mind that waiting has no object. For, the moment one knows what, or whom, one is waiting for, waiting has already ended: one is already in expectancy, where arrival is the mere actualisation, where waiting is only a phase. Moreover, if one already knows the object that, whom, one is waiting for, (s)he, it, is always already there — and one is in mere chronological time; where the object has already arrived and is just not yet materialised. But, at the same time, if one has absolutely no idea of what, or whom, one is waiting for, there is no relationality, there is no waiting as well. Thus, the only way in which one can be waiting — without it being just functional, simply utilitarian — is to have a name to the waiting; where one is waiting for a name, without necessarily knowing whom or what this name corresponds to, with. In this way, it is a relationality to something, but a something that remains in possibility.

Godot, for instance.

Where there is a distance, a gap between, that opens the possibility that the name that one is awaiting is not just about to come, but also perhaps always already there; an « *already* and a *not yet* ». But, not in the same form as when one knows the object: for that is when the idea is already there, and the material object not yet. This, instead, is a *radical transformation* of one's experience of waiting: where both the *eidos* and the *physis* are both simulateneously potentially there, and not yet there. Where, all one can say is that, *I wait.*[55]

Allowing all echoes of Roland Barthes' beautiful question, « Am I in love? » to resound here, alongside the, his, enigmatic response: « — Yes, since I'm waiting ».[56] And where else is that waiting but in the dash, « — », between the mark of the question, and the response. For, he continues, « the lover's identity is precisely: *I am the one that waits* ».

Which opens for us, leaves us with, the question of the « I », and the identity of this « I » : for, since the *I* cannot quite know whom, or what, (s)he might be awaiting, and since love is the openness to the possibility of another, of the possibility of the Two, all the *I* can know is that it is « the one that waits ». Whether another responds, whether another comes, whether the other that comes is *I* itself is not known; and perhaps can never be known, even if, even after, there is a response.

For, the *I love you* that one hears might always only be perhaps voices in one's head.

Which might be why one can say — at least in the English language — that *I am a faithful person*,[57] that I am a person of faith. For, faith always already brings with it a notion of doubt — without which, it is already a matter of knowledge, of knowing. In order for there to be faith, one has to acknowledge that one believes in spite of the fact that it might be untrue or, at least that, the object of one's faith might remain veiled from one. Thus, it is a relationality between one, the *I* — for to have faith, one must say that one is the one, that *it is I who have*, who professes, faith — and the object that is *already* and also *not yet* here. For, to know that *I am a faithful person*, one would both have to already be faithful to, and yet also have to wait until the end, until the end of the relationality, to know if one has been faithful. Hence, *I am a faithful person* is, and can always only be, a profession, a promise, acting as if one is faithful. And in acting as if, one lives as a faithful person; one has a *radical transformation* and is always already — even as one is not yet — faithful, can never be faithful enough.

Which is also why *I am a faithful person* is, must be, an utterance. For, it is, and cannot ever be, at the level of fact: it is only so as it is said to be. Not even a performative statement — even as it might affect another, cause another to do something, might sometimes be perlocutionary — but one which refers to nothing except its own utterance, does nothing except call itself — one's own faithfulness — into being.

And, more than that, it is an utterance that waits — that awaits the possibility of its own being, its becoming. An utterance that is faithful to the possibility of its own fidelity.

An utterance that remains faithful to itself.

One made in fidelity to nothing but the possibility of fidelity.

To write as question of writing,
question
that bears the writing
that bears the question …

—Maurice Blanchot

But a task whose solution is by the same token the object of a knowledge, a task which as a simple recognition would render accessible, would this still be a task?

— Jacques Derrida

CALL ME

CALL ME

As one is attempting to respond, write in response, write as a response, the question that continually haunts the writing is: *is one actually responding to a call*? Or more precisely, *is one responding to a call* or *is the call always already a reading, an interpretive gesture, a version of the response*: in attempting to respond to a call, are we also already writing that call into being?

In all of this, we can hear echoes of Augustine, who opens his text, *Confessions*, with a series of questions: « how can one call for what one does not recognise? Without such recognition, one could be calling for something else, Or is calling for you the way to recognise you? ».[1] Is one called, or does one have to answer a call? Or more pertinently, is there even a call if it is not answered; which is a question of, is the status of a call dependent on a response? Augustine's reflections might well have been an echo of the well-known episode in *Genesis*, where Yahweh calls out Abraham's name. The fact that Yahweh has to call twice (or even thrice depending on the version you are reading) suggests that Abraham ignores this call at least once. Which is completely understandable considering that divine calls are rarely pleasant: he turned out to be completely on the mark here — in answering the call, he had to then murder his son. The fact that Isaac was replaced at the last minute by a ram makes no difference to the fact that Abraham was ready to commit filicide. So, one should bear in mind that answering a call is always already potentially dangerous. This is, of course, not lost on the writers of scripture as the story of the Nazarene ends with another famous call — this time, a call for help. Nearing death, Jesus of Nazareth looks up to the skies and utters, « *Eloi Eloi lama sabachthani* », « My God, my god, why have you forsaken me ». An unanswered call, put on call-waiting as it were, a call that also echoes helplessness, desperation; a cry of *daddy, daddy, where the fuck are you?* Answering a call can lead to death; not having your call answered, not answering a call, might just be as fatal.

So, this was the problem facing me as I heard the call to write this text. For, since a call to write has no referent — it says nothing about what is to be written — it remains quite indiscernible as to what kind of call it is: whether an informative call, which lets one know something; a call to do something, to action; perhaps a call to stay away, to do nothing, a warning. And as the call has no object, at least potentially no known object — for, even if one responds, even if one writes, there is no necessary correspondence between what is written and what is called for — one can never be certain if one is responding to a call, the call, any call, even as one is writing, even after one has written. In other words, all attempts at responding — all of us who have attempted to respond to any call — are haunted by the possibility that one is potentially responding to a call that were merely voices in one's head.

Thus, even as there may be a response, the very status of a call as call remains beyond one, remains unknowable.

And, these thoughts were coming to me at the same time as I was pondering a conversation with my dear teacher, Avital Ronell — we had been, were, talking about phones, phone calls, and connections, during which she recounted the story that prompted her to start writing her masterpiece, *The Telephone Book*. The gist of the tale was that when asked about his involvement in the Nazi party, Martin Heidegger dismissed it — *all I did was to answer the phone call of the SA Storm-trooper*. Which was a strange response; particularly when coming from someone who had devoted his thinking to events, to possibilities, to the call of otherness. Which opened the question: *why do some calls matter, and why did others not*; alongside, *is it ever possible to dismiss a call that one has answered?*

Even a prank call.

After all, any call — even one which is inadvertently picked up — can affect one's day.

And this was the lesson that Jacques Derrida, Avital's teacher, never lets us forget: for, even as he had rejected the call, as it could not have been Heidegger who was already dead — thus never discovering, uncovering, the identity of the person who made the

I must note it right here, on the morning of 22 August 1979, 10 A.M., while typing this page for publication, the telephone rings. The U.S. The American operator asks me if I accept a 'collect call' from Martin (she says Martine or martini) Heidegger. I heard, as one often does in these situations which are very familiar to me, often having to call "collect" myself, voices that I

said call, who attempted to contact him — for the rest of the night, and clearly for a long time afterwards, he was affected by the call. Moreover, it is not as if any of us can immunise ourselves from such potential effects: even in this day of caller identification technology, one can never know for sure who is on the other line until one picks up. And even if one did know who was calling, one can never quite be sure what the call is — no one ever said you'd like what you hear. To compound matters, as the prank call to Derrida is immortalised in print, until his death in 2004, he potentially opened himself to being asked about this call, opened himself to being called again, as it were, by Heidegger.[2]

But perhaps, for a moment, we should take Martin Heidegger at his word, and consider the possibility of him *answering a call but not-answering* at the same time. A performative answer, as it were.

thought I recognised
on the other end of the
intercontinental line,
listening to me and
watching my reaction.
What will he do with the
ghost or Geist of Martin?
I cannot summarise here
all the chemistry of the
calculation that very
quickly made me refuse
("It's a joke, I do not
accept") after having the
name Martini Heidegger
repeated several times,
hoping that the author
of the farce would finally
name himself. Who pays,
in sum, the addressee or
the sender? who is to pay?
This is a very difficult
question, but this morning
I thought, I should not
pay, at least not otherwise
than by adding this note of
thanks.

— Jacques Derrida

After all, such utterances escape our lips numerous times daily: 'how are you', 'how's it going', are not genuine questions; and it is not as if the one asking actually cares, or even want an answer. However, it is not as if one can get away without answering; even if one knows that the question was not quite, wasn't actually, seeking an answer. For, failure to respond would shatter the very code we live in, live by, the rules, and laws that form our culture. And when we speak of laws, the spectre of Kafka is never far behind: so, even as we perhaps stand before the law — even if we are completely aware that it governs us, judges us — this does not mean that we know what, or whom, this law is. At the end of this particular road lies a velvet curtain that reveals perhaps absolutely nothing; more terrifyingly, if there is no man pulling the ropes, the wizard might well have always been oneself. After all, something only becomes cultural when it is repeated endlessly: until the point when one is no longer cognisant of why the particular repetition even happens in the first place. Something is cultural when ritualised: devoid of meaning except for the very act itself. Repeated for its own sake. And here, it is not too difficult to hear Avi's teaching that there is no culture without addiction: repetitions that we have become hooked on; where you shoot up on these particular motions, sayings, actions — our daily dose of courtesy. And whenever we hear habit, the notion of *habitus*, our own bodies, is never too far away. Why some addictions are legitimate, acceptable, whilst others are not is another story: after all, all of them can hijack your life, derail you, seize you, and very well cause you to cease being you.

And here, we should take the notion of story itself seriously: for, all narratives are bound by laws, regulations, expectations; all stories are set in, within the confines of, a genre. Including stories about oneself, your life story, stories one tells oneself. But, since there is quite possibly no one behind that curtain, the voice of the law, the voice that calls out to one, might well be one calling to oneself.

Imagine what Isaac would say if no one actually asked his daddy to kill him. No wonder Isaac — *Yitzhak* — was named laughter: what else can you do when daddy is trying to cleft thee in twain.

And since we can never be sure of the status of a response — of whether one is responding to the call of another, or whether it is a response to a call made by oneself — we have to consider if the attempt to respond is also a call. Of whether responding to another is a call in itself; a calling out to the other whom one is responding to, and with. Here, we can hear echoes of Lucretius' conception of communication; which he envisages as a coming together of atoms from one body to another: these atoms meet in the skin in-between, the *simulacra*, where they react to, alter, each other. This suggests that it is two-way insofar as there has to be more than one body involved, but at the same time the manner in which the bodies involved are affected remains singular. More importantly, the outcome of the communion — the manner in which the bodies

To conceive:

1. to bring forth something into the world

2. where this thing comes from one, from within one

3. yet, at the very same time, was also inseminated into one, from beyond one

Where communication is quite possibly not just a *naissance* but — since one never quite knows, can never truly know from whence it comes — always also *an immaculate conception.*

respond with each other — is unknown until it happens; an emergent property, as it were. Which means that every act of communication is a potential risk; where, even if in relation to, in a relationality with, a performative question, the response of the other might just resound in you. This risk that we encounter in each act of communication — the meeting, mingling, and negotiation, between atoms — only happens at the moment of communication; the interaction between the two happens in a moment. Thus, communication and time are inseparable. Communication is a communion in time: one where all bodies involved *do this in memory of me.* For, in order to communicate, all bodies have to rely on a common code — learnt through mimesis; where the habit inhabits one's *habitus*. But the manner in which the coming together affects the bodies, perhaps even the code itself, remains unknowable till it happens: which suggests that each communion is not only in memory, of memory, but also potentially a resurrection of the possibility of communion, and a transubstantiation of communicability itself. So, even as one is doing this through memory, one is always potentially re-writing memory itself. Where, not only do the bodies involved possibly alter, each communion might alter what we call communication itself.

Doing in memory of
|
resurrecting memory
|
rewriting memory
|
remembering memory

Which brings us to the time and space we are in right now. For, if each moment of communication is possibly an event, it is always already a work-in-progress, not in any linear sense of 'this is all that I have done prior to this, and this is where it is going' but, in the very thinking of what is being written, read — that is the 'work' — as it is being communicated. And here, one cannot but hear the echo of community in communication: after all, one cannot be in communion alone. Which suggests that each and every person gathered here today, in reading, in writing, all of our phantom readers, writers, editors — our congregation as it were — is part of the work that is being thought of, meditated on — called; where, one might even go so far as to posit that communion and thought go hand in hand. For, even if one attempts to think about something in one's own time, one is already calling out to the others, all others, who have thought about, and are thinking about, might possibly, at some point, be thinking about, the same notion.

... Call me (call me) on the line/ Call me, call me any, anytime/ Call me (call me) my love/ You can call me any day or night/ Call me ...

— Blondie

In this manner, any call is not just a call for a presentation by one to others; it is an invitation for a gathering, for community itself. And in all calls, one can — if one listens carefully — hear echoes of another call, one that was sent forth in 1980 by Deborah Harry and Giorgio Moroder.

Thus, in responding, in attending, to a call, one is not just answering, but more importantly, one is putting forth one's own call — a call that doesn't pretend to know what, or whom, it is responding to, or even what it may be thinking about, a call that might not have an object, let alone an objective, to it, but a call that invites another, each other, perhaps all others, even those that are not here, to call us, to callings, to thought.

In fidelity to nothing but quite possibly the possibility of calls — of responding to calls.

Why is the call thought of as something which, rather than taken, taken down, or taken in — be it from a specific agent, subject, principle, preferably a moral one — will be given? And if each call which issues is destined to make demands on the one who is called (but this is also questionable), is it already settled that I will hear, that I will hear this call and hear it as one destined for me? Is it not rather the case that the minimal condition to be able to hear something as something lies in my comprehending it neither as destined for me nor as somehow oriented toward someone else? Because I would not need to hear it in the first place if the source and destination of the call, of the call as call, were already certain and determined. Following the logic of calling up, of the call … and along with that the logic of demand, of obligation, of law, no call can reach its addressee simply as itself, and each hearing is consummated in the realm of the possibility not so much of hearing as being able

Does one write about something because one knows something — or absolutely nothing — about it?

Where, responding to a call means that one has to always already be unfaithful to every other possible call.

Which is also the question of: *is a call, a call to intelligence, to listen up by ceasing to hear. Hearing ceases. It listens to a noise, a sound, a call; and so hearing always ceases hearing, because it could not let itself be determined other than as hearing, to hearing any further. Hearing ceases. Always. Listen …*

— Werner Hamacher

the intelligent,
a call to make
intelligible, or
is it always
already that of
the unknown,
the unknowable,
a call to the
stupid, to
stupidity.

I cannot be in any relationship. For to do so, I would have to be unfaithful to myself…

—Avital Ronell

Plagiarism is the foundation of all literatures except the first, which is unknown.

— Jean Giraudoux

Keeping in mind that the first,
the *protos*, can change (*proteus*),
is always already changing.

I, WHO WE'AKENED

•••

I, WHO WEAKENED ...

I never loved nobody fully
Always one foot on the ground
And by protecting my heart truly
I got lost in the sounds ....

— Regina Spektor

I saw you one morning. Standing there.
I hadn't known that you had already fallen for me.
I barely even knew who you were.
That is, until the chief came up to me.
With eleven hundred shekels no less.

At least she got to say, *wherefore art thou ...*
At least she got to ask.
All they told me was: *think of it as a gift, nothing more.*

Compressing me

'Till this day I'm not sure if it was mere vanity. Rumour has it that he likes women he wasn't supposed to. Perhaps, I was just another.

Nor had I known that his god acted through him. So, I'll never know if he actually loved me. I do think though, he did. They claim — their book claims — that he only told me his secret « after he grew tired to death » of me questioning him.[1] But, they weren't there were they — *these scribes, these Pharisees.*

Wallpaper

Do walls have ears? Perhaps they heard; perhaps the scribes imagine they heard, are writing what they think they heard. And one of them — pricking up his ears, picking up his reed, (what a prick!) — inscribed.

Perhaps, he writes what
he thinks he heard
happened on the bed.
Thus, a writing — that is
to say, a reading of what
he thinks he heard.

Peut-être, il écrit ce qu'il
pense avoir entendu se
passer sur le lit. Ainsi, une
écriture — c'est-à-dire, une
lecture de ce qu'il pense,
avoir entendu.

That now, you read.
Or, perhaps, what I read.
All on a bed.

Que maintenant, tu lis.
Ou, peut-être, que je lis.
Tout sur un lit.

Beneath these sheets of paper lies my truth.

— Regina Spektor

Who would ever grow tired of defending the secret to one's power, his strength? None of you would have managed to tame him if not for me. I was the one who finally teased the secret from him. Without force, without trickery even.

For, he knew.

And gave it to me. On the fourth time — perhaps this was his way of testing me; perhaps even, his way of teasing me. But certainly, an act of love — for love.

For, no one betrays his god — except for love. Is there any other way to betray the jealous one other than through loving another, by love for another, by loving another.

Not that this would make any difference.

For, it is not as if one is jealous of something: jealously is *a priori*, is about holding on to, seizing, grasping, making claims on, owning, knowing, claiming to know, claiming knowledge over.
Thus, whether there is another that is loved or not is irrelevant — in jealously, there is no longer any other; perhaps not even the one whom the jealous one claims to love.

Which might be why the feminine has always been what power is most afraid of. For, in its reversibility, it foregrounds — makes clear, all too clear — the lesson of Søren Kierkegaard:

> *"My" — what does the word designate? Not what belongs to me, but what I belong to, what contains my whole being, which is mine insofar as I belong to it.*

And, that there is never any reason — keeping in mind that measurement, *ratio*, proportion, specifications, forms, checklists, accounting, limitations, delimitations, exclusion, is precisely the very hinge around which power revolves — for jealousy.

That one is jealous because one is jealous.

And when faced with this challenge — not an opposition, for that would be too easy to deal with but — a challenge to its very security, stability, stasis, status, as power, to power as power itself, what else can it do but lash out: what else does it do but turn to terror.

Turn to, become, precisely what it is not.

For, we should try not to forget that even as they may seem similar, power and terror are completely different: whilst the former is a contest of wills

Masculinity has always been haunted by this sudden reversibility within the feminine. Seduction and femininity

between parties, the alterity of the parties remain; terror is the complete effacement of the other by one; terror is when there is no other.

Yahweh's
jealousy.

are ineluctable as the reverse side of sex, meaning, and power.

— Jean Baudrillard

So before, they come and break down the door ...

The continual testing of Samson's love. That he might actually have wanted to share his secret, the secret; the pact between him and his god with another. And for that, Yahweh « turned away from him ».

***

Centuries later, someone would finally understand:

I loved you first.

Even before you asked.
I don't deny that I already knew of you, had known your name, of your name. Who didn't.
So, when they told me your name, the name of the one I had to bring down, weaken, it was a name that had already sung to me many times before. And perhaps, the moment I knew your name, your name also knew me.

I heard there

was a secret

chord

that David

played and it

pleased the Lord

— Leonard Cohen

Perhaps then, it was only appropriate that it had resurrected — perhaps, the only way *I loved you first* could only have reemerged was — in a song.

Can one fall in love with a name?
Can one ever name one whom one has fallen in love with?
Can one ever do anything other than name the one that one has fallen in love with?
Is love a — another — name for falling?
Is naming all one can do as one falls?

Perhaps

love —

falling.

each

already

can never

with

love; or if

What is the sound of a name?

Perhaps, the sound that is made as it is uttered, as one utters the name; even if not audibly, even if one's utterance is inaudible; perhaps only for, to, oneself.

Or even, the name that one is called, that one calls another — the name that calls out to us.

Perhaps — nothing but a sound that calls to us. For, who said that a name had to have anything to do with another, any other.

that is the very relationality that is the relationship between itself and Not that they are separable from other, but that they are always also other to each other. Where you quite be sure if one is falling in love another; or if one is falling in(to) love is the very falling itself.

Perhaps, this is why all you know, can ever know, is what has been told to you, was written by, the scribes, the Pharisees. For, you only know — will always only know — him as Samson.

I have my own name, sound, for him.

... but you don't really care for music do 'ya.

My very own — secret chord.

***

Samson — hero of his people.
Samson — scourge of his enemies. A judge of his people; one who judges his enemies, judges others, judges the others, judges us.
Wields his authority.

Plays daddy.
Plays at being daddy.

But, let no one forget that the prophecy
— the prophecy of him, his prophecy —
was for women, only came through a woman.

For, the angel appeared to his mother.

And only when summoned — by her — did Manoah, her husband, did he, get to speak with the angel. And — unlike her — he did not even recognise who he was speaking with until much later, 'till « the flame went up heavenwards from the altar »,[3] 'till it was painfully obvious. But even then, even after all that, she remains nameless, the angel remains unknown — « Why ask my name? It is a mystery ».[4]

Perhaps a mystery can only come through one that remains mysterious, one who remains nameless — perhaps even a remainder.

A conduit — without which, nothing could have happened.

Keeping in mind that mysteries are, the truly mysterious is, what makes us tremble. Leaves us — perhaps only temporarily, but certainly at least momentarily — weakened.

And here, we should try not to forget that one can only tremble at a mystery — that a mystery can only cause one to tremble — if it is first recognised as a mystery; if one first catches a glimpse of the possibility that it is, that something might be, mysterious.

Perhaps only when one names it as a mystery; perhaps at the point when one responds to the potentiality of its mystery calling out to one.

Where trembling might well be its sound.

Just like me.

I'd like to think that when he pushed down the pillars, he evoked my name — that as they fell, echoes of my name were ringing throughout the hall.

That as he commended his spirit into the hands of his father — « Lord Yahweh, I beg you, remember me; give me strength this once, and let me be revenged on the Philistines at one blow for my two eyes »[5] — the answer was *weakness.*

Not just of the pillars; not just of the Nazirite who had to acknowledge that he was always only a medium; but that he was the *man of the sun* only at the moment when he let the light shine through, only when he got out of the way, only when he was weakened.

I don't believe in an interventionist God
But I know, darling, that you do
But if I did I would kneel down and ask Him
Not to intervene when it came to you
Not to touch a hair on your head
To leave you as you are
And if He felt He had to direct you Then direct you into my arms

— Nick Cave

That the key to his strength,
— the *cipher*,
the secret to his power —
was not his hair,
but his obedience.

In bowing before; in being nothing.

For, he had no way of knowing if Yahweh had forgotten him or not, would return him his strength by re-membering him. Or, might just ignore him, turn his face away from him.[6] The only thing that Samson knew was that he was dead: either through the building falling on him, or by the hands of the Philistines who would have killed him for attempting to murder them. His only request, — « may I » — was to « die with the Philistines ».[7]

And it is only through becoming nothing — embracing death before dying — that « those he killed at his death outnumbered those he had killed in his life ».[8]

The philosophers might even say: by encountering death before dying, he had come as close to god as one can. So not just becoming nothing then — but perhaps, even nothingness.

But not to me.

On love — or, on falling.
Whilst never quite knowing,
being able to know, not just at the point of the fall, whilst one is falling, but perhaps even after the fall why — or even for whom, let alone who — one has fallen.

Before the fall: She does not know that she is naked. A nakedness so unsexual that the part of her body which (always) very early on gave me prudish horror, — was her toes, especially the big one, and about her feet — which paints her soul. Psychic feet. Dense.

Like her hair —

— Hélène Cixous

Perhaps never stopping to consider that my secret was quite possibly also in my hair.

That perhaps I was the chosen one as my people suspected there was a possibility that Samson might just « like her hair ».[9]
And perhaps, just as my Nazirite was shorn of his locks, I was of my tale. Of my tale with him.
Of our story.

Delilah

'temptress, treacherous lover,' taken from the name of the woman who seduced and betrayed Samson in the book of *Judges*;

from the Hebrew *Delilah*, literally 'delicate, languishing, amorous';

from the Semitic root *d-l-l* — 'to hang down, to languish.'

Shorn not
just of my
tale.

But, my
very
name.

So perhaps, as I write, all that I am attempting to do is to — all that I write is an attempt to respond — listen to, the *d-l-l*, to languish in the delicateness of the relation between the two; the relationship that Yahweh attempts to intrude upon, trample over, exert himself onto.

Perhaps then, nothing but an attempt to dwell in the possibility that I was delectable, that despite all the warnings from his god, Samson was willing to dwindle away, to be imprisoned between pillars, be made to « amuse »[10] my people in their dwellings, be weakened, left dangling. For perhaps — and this I can only hope — he knew, always knows, that even as his god might have « turned away from him »,[11] the one who is dear to him, the one who calls him her darling, never would, perhaps never will.

That, even if you refuse us the possibility of love, that at least

*For those, however, who would not regard gl as a satisfactory response — since they expected some response in the first place; those for whom gl says nothing — since they believed gl was saying nothing in the first place — and who, one wonders for what meal [*repas*], would continue to drool on the spot [*sur place*], let us suggest that the theoretical question, elaborated surely (metalangue — that always reconstitutes itself — in the better place) by this intervention, no other word is possible today, submitted in advance to the censorship of the remain(s), after all, in the ideological field, will produce, that's how (*comme ça*) it has to be said, the following thesis: every thesis is (bands erect) a prosthesis; what affords reading affords reading by citations (necessarily truncated, clippings [*coupures*],*

you give us the leeway that we had « become infatuated. With another ». Keeping in mind that « this does not happen without profit or loss for the both of us that have undergone grafting, who have been inextricably altered, after having been solicited, collared [*racoler*] ».

And « those, however, who would not regard an attempt to respond to the sound of my name as a satisfactory response — since they expected some response in the first place; those for whom sound says nothing — since they believed sound was saying nothing in the first place — … let us suggest that the theoretical question, elaborated surely … by this intervention, no other word is possible today, submitted in advance to the censorship of the remain(s), after all, in the ideological field, will produce, that's how (*comme ça*) it has to be said, the following thesis: every thesis is (bands erect) a prosthesis;

repetitions, suctions, sections, suspensions, selections, stitchings [coutures]*, scarrings, grafts, postiches, organs without their own proper body, proper body covered with cuts* [coups]*, traversed by lice). Thus, does a text become infatuated. With another. This does not happen without profit or loss for the organism that undergoes grafting after having been solicited, collared* [racoler]*.*

— Jacques Derrida

what affords reading
affords reading by citations
(necessarily truncated,
clippings [*coupures*],
repetitions, suctions, sections,
suspensions, selections,
stitchings [*coutures*],
scarrings, grafts, postiches,
organs without their own
proper body, proper body
covered with cuts [*coups*],
traversed by lice) ».[12]

So, perhaps the only meaning — if you are still looking for some — that might come from this writing, this reading, this reading of my writing, a writing that perhaps takes the voice from another, even as it may purport to, even attempt to, be listening, responding — but what writing doesn't always already — is the sound that comes with my name, a sound grafted from another sound, another song, from a different time, a different voice, one between the time of those scribes, those who write to efface, and other scribes, those who write your name in an attempt to tell our tale, to one that might perhaps be a voice in-between, one who was telling the tale of perhaps another with my name, but in doing so, might well have caught a glimpse, allowed us to hear a whisper, of the question that is raised by my name. A question that continues to haunt this tale, both mine and yours: for, after all, no one will really know the reason you gave up your power; no one will know mine, none of you ever even know where those eleven hundred shekles went …

Perhaps all that is left, the sound that is left to us is; perhaps the sound that continued, continues, to haunt the scribes who have all attempted to explicate, explain away, reason even, provide meaning where there might be none in their own way — by effacing, by re-telling, by interpreting, by analysis, by re-writing — is,

why
why
why
Delilah ...

So, perhaps a writing that is nothing but an attempt to respond to a call, a call from elsewhere, from a time that has naught to do with the moment, time, tale, that I am attempting to write about — a call that I had happened to read, had read, and perhaps in that small way opened myself to being called by it. To be seduced by its call: and in that very moment of being opened, in that very opening, perhaps momentarily been weakened.

Write a narrative in which the speaker starts to understand that events, as they happen in her/ his life, can be seen not as surprises but as an uncovering — the systematic revelation of fate.

— Chris Kraus

Whilst, always already running the risk that the Delilah
I am attempting — maybe even helping — to uncover,
perhaps unveil (*dévoiler*),
take flight (*voler*), escape,
is only the one of my reading:
is only my Delilah.

Feel free to notice that the attitude we would have liked to adopt — with a view to, or perhaps, with a foreknowledge of the desired end of the story — has led us to the discovery of a given psychological world that supports the idea of freedom of choice; but as soon as the progression of the story requires one or the other of its main characters to pronounce a judgement, to take thought, we are immediately confronted by the arbitrary: the character escapes from its author, becoming its own singular being. Thus, we have to admit that the author is able to reveal certain traits of this character only after the fact ...

Scenting (the word seems most accurate) ...

— Jean Genet

CE N'EST PAS UN CALMAR

CE N'EST PAS UN CALMAR

At the point when I was stuck, when I felt that I could no longer go on writing, when the proverbial ink was no longer flowing, I starting walking, moving around — in an attempt to leave, if only momentarily, if only in my mind, the « room of phantoms », as Robert Walser might say.[1] For, as my dear teacher — Avital Ronell — always reminded me, one has to keep in mind, respect the possibility that, the movement of thought and our bodies are potentially entwined. That since thought quite possibly moves, we might have to move along to it, perhaps with it. A moving that we were attempting during many of our walks; for, many of her teaching moments were conducted as we were walking in, meandering through, the woods of Saas Fee.

A walk that was always a little away, apart from the maddening crowd. A walk that was also away from the trails that Saas Fee itself is known for: the paths up the mountains that echo with the footsteps of Rousseau, Zarathustra, the monster who adopts yet declines the name of Frankenstein, Byron, Shelley, Mary Wollstonecraft Godwin, Nietzsche, amongst many others.

Thinking with a little distance from everyone else, all else.

For, one must never forget that the role of the teacher is distinctly anti-public, *anti polis*. As Socrates reminds us, the role of philosophy is the corruption of youth; not by turning them away from what is good — for, the one who loves wisdom is also a lover of beauty, truth — but by opening the love of wisdom, by opening thought, thinking, questioning, in them. And *love* in the specific sense of *philia*: two way, in relation with, whilst never claiming to fully know another, whilst being open to the possibility of the other. Which suggests that this is a relationality that is reasoned, reasonable, within the boundaries of rationality; but at the same time always also open to the unknown, the potentially unknown, to the potentiality of unknowability. For, we must not forget that even though this is a relationship of love, it is not haphazard, not completely reliant on chance: there is craft, discipline, *tekhnē*, involved. But even as there is craft in thinking, even as there is method in this journey of thought (*meta hodos*; over a path), Socrates teaches us that wisdom only comes to one from elsewhere, from beyond; only comes to one at the point where the *daemon* whispers in one's ear. Which means that even as one can attempt to teach another, that even as one might be able to be taught, be open to the possibility of being taught, the teaching is limited to the manner in which one might approach wisdom — one is not, perhaps cannot be, taught wisdom as such.

And if teaching, and learning, involves approach, involves craft, this suggests that it requires much practice; that it is only through constant repetition that one might even begin to develop the skills required to open oneself to the possibility of the whisper. For, as Socrates never lets us forget, at the point when one hears the *daemon*, it is the craft that becomes art — nothing is said of the craftsman.

There is no artist; only the gestures of the possibility of art.

At the point of wisdom, there is no teacher; only gestures of the possibility of teaching.

Which is why Avi didn't — never sought to — tell, to impose upon, to impart even, but instead always only conducted the flow of our thoughts as we moved — listening to its rhythm, its rises and falls, its tempo, its time. For, we should try to not forget that the teacher — the *pedagogue* — only can guide, lead (*agogos*; leader) the ones (*paida*; boy) being taught. Thus, it is not a direct transference of information, or even knowledge, but a leading by example. Where the very habits of the teacher — and by extension the teacher's body (*habitus*) — is the very site of the teaching. Which is why Martin Heidegger teaches us that, « the real teacher, in fact, lets nothing else be learned than — learning. His conduct, therefore, often produces the impression that we properly learn nothing from him, if by 'learning' we now suddenly understand merely the procurement of useful information. The teacher is ahead of his apprentices in this alone, that he has still far more to learn than they — he has to learn to let them learn. The teacher must be capable of being more teachable than the apprentices. The teacher is far less assured of his ground that those who learn are of theirs ».[2]

Her too, Martin — always her as well.

Thus, the teacher and the student are in a relationality, where they are open to the possibility of learning — and the site of this potential learning is in, on, their bodies.

Which brings us back to *love.*

And the fact that love itself is the very condition of learning.

In the precise sense that even as the one who teaches professes — allowing all echoes of faith, unknowability, whispers of the divine even, to resound here — (s)he is always also always an amateur. The one who teaches is the one that loves, is one in love (*amore*).

Bearing in mind that love always entails a risk — it is never safe, and the one in love opens herself, subjects himself, to its dangers.

And, at this juncture, if your spidey-senses are tingling, and alarm-bells are going off about the possibility that we are encroaching dangerously close to the terrain of *paedophilia* — they should be. For, if love is the premise of learning, of teaching, one should bear in mind that teaching, learning, quite possibily always already entails a fall — where the ones involved potentially do what they otherwise might not have, perhaps transgress not just mores, norms, but their very selves. Where to be in love is to open oneself — with all that it entails.

Which is not to say that teaching always entails sex, or expensive gifts. Far from it. After all, discernment, choice, saying no, is a mark of intelligence.

However, just because we discriminate, select, does not mean that we are not open to possibilities, does not entail an *a priori* dismissal. For, an intelligent choice can only be made after considering, consideration, after a certain care is taken to think — which means, only after the possibility that one is open to something, to someone, is first considered.

Care:

particularly when the teaching is in a seminar. Bearing in mind that in a seminary one germinates, grows, trims, cuts, prunes, disseminates, quite possibly inseminates. Thus perhaps — whether one likes it or not — to teach, if by teaching we mean opening our students and ourselves to possibilities, even if one is taking all care to say no, is to always already fuck one's student; insofar as one is always also being fucked by her, him, them.

Thus, a categorical dismissal of the potential relationality between a student and a teacher — even if this relationship extends to a sexual nature — is to make teaching a profession, to divorce it from *amore*, love. Which is not just to sterilise the one who teaches — it is the devastation of the possibility of thought itself.

And if openness to possibility is one of the conditions of thought, this also suggests that to think, one has to potentially be open to the very notion, question, of thinking itself: *one has to think without — before — knowing what thinking itself is.*

Thinking without thinking, as it were; or, more precisely, thinking without deciding that it is — perhaps without naming it — thinking.

Perhaps then, thinking as openness to the possibility of thinking. Without thinking that one knows, that one has been taught, what thinking is.

Thus, a thinking that is before, beyond, and also open, to thinking. And yet, only happens as one is thinking.

Le pas au-dela.

And here, we should also attempt to bear in mind that the risk entailed when learning is not just to one's mind, but potentially also to one's body: for, as one practices one's craft, as one constantly repeats, as one builds certain habits, these write themselves onto, shape our, *habitus*, bodies.

Which means that at the point in which we have learnt, the point when it becomes a habit, we might also forget that we have been learning. For, we only know that we truly know something when it becomes instinctive, when we no longer have to think about it, when it becomes second nature — perhaps not secondary to our nature, but another nature, a nature that has somehow been opened in us, inscribed onto us, written into us.

Which also means that we can never quite know if we truly know. That truly knowing is always already also unknowable, might well lie in the unknown.

Thus, perhaps it is not just that knowing that we know is unknowable, but that unknowability is not only the limit but always also the condition of knowledge itself. That the foundation — or *abgrund*, if you prefer — of knowledge is its unknown; where unknowability is not its opposite, its antonym, but its own foregrounding of its limits each time it professes, testifies to its knowing, to knowledge. Which means that each profession of knowledge is always also knowledge testifying to itself, telling its self, bringing itself forth — attempting to narrate what it is.

Thus, always also a moment of fiction, literature.

A writing of itself.

Which suggests that first and foremost, in order to know — leaving aside whether it is even, ever, possible to know that one knows — one has to first and foremost read. And not a reading that attempts to decode, that aims at being definitive, concrete, static, that aims at certainty, tries to be certain; but reading as the openness to the possiblity of not just the text, not just to what is being read, but reading itself. A reading that might well still be a kind of hermeneutics but which bears in mind that Hermes can never quite be caught; and, perhaps more importantly, that it is Hermes who brings the message — what is being read — to one; thus, always

This suggests that reading can no longer be constituted in the classical tradition of hermeneutics, as an act of deciphering meaning according to a determined set of rules, laws: this would be reading as an act where the reader comes into a convergence at best with the text. In fact, reading can no longer be understood as an act, since an act by necessity be governed by the rules of reading. Reading must be thought as the event of an encounter with an other — an other who is not the other as identified by the reader, but rather an other that remains beyond the cognition of the self.

also, a message that might well not be from the text, or at least is not solely from the text. That, even as one is reading, one remains blind, perhaps also deaf, to both the source and foundation of one's reading.[3]

Thus, a reading that cannot know itself, cannot know if it is even reading.

A reading that might well be writing itself, crafting itself — being crafty — as one is reading. Which suggests that it is not that nothing happens when one reads, but that the only thing that happens is reading: the *tekhnē* that brings forth is not just what is being read but reading itself.

Hence reading is a pre-relational relationality: an encounter with the other without any claims to knowing who or what this other is in the first place: an unconditional relation, and a relation to no fixed object of relation. As such, it is the ethical moment par excellence.

— Jeremy Fernando

Therefore, when one speaks of *a love of reading, a love for literature*, it is not just that it has to be cultivated, nurtured, in people through enjoyment, pleasure, rather than by focusing on utility, need, value, least of all use-value, but that reading, literature itself, is fundamentally useless.

Which is why those in power have always been fearful of it: and here, one should never forget that the first to be shot are always poets and writers. Not because they actually do anything, but that precisely by doing nothing they give, open, the space for us to imagine something else, something other. And if literature is entwined with use, if one insists on entwining literature with utility, all that is done is to tie it down, enchain it, to the state. Ironically, those that claim to love literature are the ones who tend to have done the most violence to it. We can hear this resound in common complaints such as: *we should be taken more seriously*; *I wish people would stop saying that we only read story books*; *we are transmitting important life skills to our students*, amongst others.

Attempts at, gestures towards, *gravitas*.

But, what else is literature but the reading of stories. Which is not to say that stories are only found in books. However, what is crucial is the love for stories: and this is learned, developed, through an attention towards, a love of, for, books. And here, one should not forget the echoes of *book* and *learning* that can be heard in literature (from the Old English *boccræft*) — alongside registers of *mimesis*, repetition, habit, and *habitus*.

Or, as another teacher of mine, Neil Murphy, might say: *show me what you read and I'll tell you who you are*.

For, we are always already in a relationality with what we read. Even before reading happens — prior to the act of reading — one has to open oneself to the possibility of reading, open oneself to reading itself. Without necessarily knowing what reading even is. Thus, to claim that literature has a use is to diminish it, shackle it to value, production, logic, *ratio*, reason.

It is to do nothing other than to attempt to erase literature. Which is not to say that literature has no effects on one.

But, that is not its point. What happens — what affects us — is after, or at best during, reading; and this is not where literature as such lies. For, literature lies in *letters* (*littera*); and like all writing, it is of the order of death.

Thus, to love literature is to be in love with the dead.

Necrophilia.

Keeping in mind that to love is to be in a relationality that, as Alain Badiou teaches us, « encompasses the experience of the possible transition from the pure randomness of chance to a state that has universal value ». Which is not to diminish « pure randomness » ; on the contrary, the very possibility of love rests on it, hinges on taking a « chance ».

And the gamble that is taken each time one picks up a book, the risk one runs in attempting to attend to a text, is the possibility of *falling* — along with all the potential disasters this entails — in love.

Thus, the stake in literature is one's very own self.

For, if writing is of the order of death, reading is openness to the possibility of resurrection.

And more than that: if literature is a love of the dead, opening ourselves to death is an openness to the unknown, and potentially always already unknowable. Perhaps this scares us, and it should. This is quite possibly why Milan Kundera calls it the *unbearable lightness of being*: it is the refusal to be grounded, to be pinned down, known, that is unbearable, that continually provokes us, challenges us, quite possibly even tears us apart. So perhaps then: the point of literature is its very poking, puncturing, potential rupturing.

And perhaps, it is symptomatic that there is allegedly a *crisis* in literature, an ignoring of literature, at the very moment when notions of identity, nationality, the nation state itself, are being questioned, called into question. For, if literature is about love for the unknown, possibilities, then it is of the order of difference rather than identification, sameness.

In other words, literature is always *anti-stasis*, anti-state.

And more than that, it is always also a challenge to the self, to our selves: it is a call to attend to the possibility of another, of something that is more important than one is, than we are, than the « I » is.

And like any call, it might well lead us to dash ourselves on the rocks.

Herein lies its danger.

And its beauty.

***

And these relationalities, questions, were continually haunting me as I was struggling to write. For, even as I was attempting to start, rev-up, kick-start, my writing with walking, one of the sound-tracks that I was hearing, that I could not get out of my mind, that was on constantly loop in the background, was that I was not good enough, that I should go somewhere else with what I was going to write, with what I had not even written — that I should just stop writing and take a hike. After all, those of us who write constantly put ourselves before the law: even willingly submit ourselves — for instance, when writing a thesis, during a dissertation process, in an attempt to send in a book proposal — to some kind of masochistic contract. And also to a publishing industry, linked somewhat to a job market, some sort of hierarchical, institutional system, where we are judged, unceasingly examined — but at the same time know not who judges us: so there is no recourse to, no real appeal against, the judgement. And should one ever raise a complaint, one is told that *this is the path that you have chosen*, that you have to *walk the walk*, that it is *this way or the highway*.

But still, regardless of the trials that one might be facing on one's walks, one must also bear in mind that even as one is able to walk, to move around, attempt to roam, there are many who can no longer walk, who no longer feel safe to walk, who are not allowed to walk. From Trayvon Martin, who's walk, who's movement, was seen, construed — vindictively, racially, perhaps even stupidly — as a threat; to Michael Brown, who was told where he could or could not walk, ordered to stop walking, to get off the middle of the road; to civil-rights marches that are cordoned, shepherded, uncivilly beaten, violently attacked; to assemblies — in Mexico, Greece, Oakland, Hong Kong, amongst many many others — that are threatened, charged upon, brutally dispersed in order to make way for certain kinds of movements that are authorised, approved, sanctioned; to refugees who are told that their presence is, their very footsteps on lands are, illegal, who are thrown into processing centres, treated like non-humans, kept barely alive, just *bare life*; to everyday occurrences where some people are, where one is, told to move faster, move slower, to get out of the way.

Which is not to say that one should ever ask, apply, for permission to walk, or to stop walking: after all, it is — at least should be, one's right to move, to walk. But that even as walking, moving, movement, and thinking, are related, have a relation with each other, this relationality can be coopted, swallowed, perhaps digested, turned back upon us — where instead of choosing to move, we are moved, shifted, shafted; where instead of thinking, we are herded, flocked, maneuvered, into unthinking.

And these spectres were replaying in me even as I was constantly *proposing resolutely that I shall soon sketch and write down in a piece or sort of fantasy, which I shall entitle 'Ce n'est pas un calmar'*.[5] Even as I was continually trying to keep in mind — to remember, call to mind, to recall, Avi's other reminder — that oftentimes one finds breakthroughs, possibilities, in what is closest, in the everyday.

For, during one of our walks — teaching-walks, teaching as walking, walking to teach — she reminded me to trust my instincts whenever I was trying to, preparing to, write. And that sometimes the books that happen to be lying on my table, the texts that I had brought in front of me — without necessarily knowing why, without necessarily even being conscious of that decision to do so, of the act of doing so — might offer me an opening into what I was attempting to think about, meditate on. That sometimes, not only do the questions that haunt us send us on, onto, into, a quest, but that they also open the possibility, bring with them the potential openings, for our response to, our responding with, them — that perhaps the questions that have been opened were opened with them, quite possibly before them, or perhaps even by them.

That sometimes all I had to do was to trust that what I was looking for was always already in front of me; that I had yet to realise that I was seeing it, that I might have only been seeing blindly.

That I might have been blind to the fact that the texts were already teaching me — as I was reading them, attempting to read them; that they might have, unbeknownst to me, already been writing onto, into, me.

Moreover, since the whisper of the *daemon* comes whenever it wishes to, there is also no reason to believe that one knows precisely whom would teach one at any point, nor if one's teacher might even be a who.

And as I was pottering around the house, I looked up and saw ….

(Yanyun Chen, *Squid Love*, 2011)

… a painting that has been hanging in front of me for the last five years, one that I have been looking at every day, especially during meals, and when I am reading — it hangs just above my dining table — a painting that is inexorably tied to, linked with, a taking in, a consumption, *la nourriture*, a nourishment, revitalisation, nurturing, certainly love, perhaps life itself even.

A painting that is ostensibly about a girl's declaration of love for, to, a squid that seems to be dead, to be lost to her, as it were. A declaration that is made in the present — « But I *still* love you » — and not a claim to some imaginary future, some impossible *always* that one tends to hear in relation to love, particularly when it comes to utterances of love. A statement that seems to suggest not just a certain intensity — of both a love and loss that is deep — but also carries with it a certain accusation: « But I still love you » ; which can quite easily be read as *since I still love you, why are you dead, why are you gone*, and perhaps more importantly, *why have you left me?* But, at the same time, it is only because the squid has left her, is no longer with her that she can make that statement: for, « the limp, wet, tentacle of a dead giant squid » is « what *remains* of love ». Not just what is left over, what stays with her after the death of the squid, but also what is *still* love — love that she is, quite literally, holding in her hands.

Opening another reading to, a literal reading of: I was *touched by love*; or even, I was *touched by your love*. And perhaps here, we should reopen our registers to Nancy's reminder of space being the condition of touch. And once the dossier of space is opened, the notion of distance is also never far behind: keeping in mind that if one and the other are in the same place, it is no longer a touching but a subsuming; a total consumption, where the other is effaced. And since the register of consumption has been brought forth, one should not forget, should not efface the fact, that for most of us, a squid is, squids are, also a source of food. And, since it is not a necessity — it would rarely be a staple for anyone — this also opens the possibility that one eats squid for pleasure, enjoyment, for the love of squid. Or perhaps even, since one is only eating a particular squid at any moment, *l'amour pour un calmar*. Not because one has to, but because one wants to, because one desires the squid. Which also suggests that there is a gap, at least a moment — a distance — between the longing to eat the squid — even as a response to the call of the squid — and one's consumption of it. And perhaps even after one physically consumes the squid — keeping in mind that desire can never be satisfied — even if the want for squid is momentarily satiated, quelled, what remains is the love, a love that is called forth, brought forth, precisely by the death of the squid, the squid that once lay in one's hands. Thus, the consumption can never be total, complete; something is always left behind, remains — but only because it was a response and not a necessity, imperative, duty. Which means that in order to be touched, there must be the possibility of refusing that touch — and more than that, the possibility that one's touch might also be refused. Even if one is touching, attempting to touch, « a limp wet tentacle of a dead giant squid ».

And perhaps, what *remains* of love, what might *still* be love, what is love, is precisely the possibility of touching.

Perhaps then, when she says « But I still love you » she is not just referring to the squid, nor just telling the squid — nor anyone else that might happen to be listening in, eavesdropping as I, and now we, have been doing — of her love for it; she is also uttering the fact that her touch, her touching of it, its touching of her, touch itself, is love.

And this is encompassed in her utterance — precisely because the « I » is always already plural. A plurality that resides in grammar itself; perhaps it is *I love* only because there is an other within the « I » ; « a plurality » that — as Maurice Blanchot teaches us — « constitutes them neither out of their own singularity nor in view of a superior unity ».[6] An « I » that is not a mark, nor a trace, of identity, but a name; keeping in mind that a name names both *one and no other* and *every other with the same name but one* at the same time. Which means that when one utters « I » it is impossible to tell whom it refers to. Moreover, the only time one has to refer to another by her proper name, the only time that one's proper name has to be used, is in the absence of the one named, in the absence of the one whom the name refers to, in the absence of the referent of the name. Thus, the « I » names nothing but the fact that it is naming, is the name for nothing but *the it that names, the it that is the name, the name that is it*. Blanchot continues: « *Le il* is not 'that one', but the neuter that marks it (as *le il* appeals to that neuter) leads it back towards the displacement without place that robs it of any grammatical place, a sort of lack in becoming between two, several or all words, thanks to which these interrupt each other, without which they would signify nothing, but which upsets them constantly to the very silence in which they extinguish themselves ».[7] And in the neuter, « it is easy to recognize in man he who is always himself and the other, the happy duality of dialogue and the possibility of communication. But it is less easy, more important perhaps, to think 'man', that is to say, also 'two', as separation that lacks unity, the leap from 0 to duality, that 1 thus giving itself as the forbidden, the between-the-two ».[8]

Where an *I love you* is always already an *I still love you*, not just in the stillness that might be required to love — the moment in which one has the possibility of uttering that it is the « I » who loves, even if this « I » is always already in between the one who utters and the one who is being loved, who is called into being as the one who is loved — but also in the fact that once uttered, there is the possibility that the utterance has called the possibility that this love is absent — that love is absence — has passed, has taken flight, *s'est envolé*. Thus, perhaps also been stolen from us, *volé de nous*: after all, the one whom we love often is *the thief of our hearts*.

Perhaps then, the « duality of dialogue and the possibility of communication » is only possible due to this « separation that lacks unity, the leap from 0 to duality » : for, if the singularity of the « I » is a stable one, then both « I » remain infinitely separated. Which is not to say that there is a complete collapse into the we: for, duality still maintains the singularity of each one, but a singularity that is not a whole, but one that is « between-the-two », a plural I that is both singular and at the same time always also open to the other, to another, that might not quite be completely separable from one.

Another that might never be separable; even if the other is already absent, having already taken flight; perhaps, having already stolen part of one even as the flight has taken place.

So, even as my receptors are screaming out *not just « man » but always also woman, Maurice,* perhaps the duality in *le il* always also brings within it, *l'elle*: even as she remains silent. Or even better, perhaps she is always already silent not because she is silenced, but that she has already taken flight — gone but not quite forgotten: always already written into *le il*.

***

Which opens the question: *how does one continue to love when the loved one is no longer there*? And perhaps even, *does, did, the loved one even, ever, have to be there in the first place?*

A question that came to me on the morning of the 18th of November, 2013, as I was sitting on a bum-boat that was chugging out to nowhere — just somewhere away from the shore, away from land, away from the writing — letter — of the law. A way from the law that might only be opened to one when one is away from one's letter, the letters known to one, one's language.

Le matin du dix-huitième jour de novembre, je m'asseyais — sur une planche, dans le petit vaisseau. Un vaisseau sans nom — ou peut-être dont je ne connaissais pas le nom. Dans un vaisseau qui m'éloignait de la terre ; transportant un vase contenant quelqu'un dont je ne connaissais pas le nom. Peut-être, quelqu'un que je tentais de connaître trente-trois ans plus tard ; pas trop tard, car il était toujours déjà trop tard. Je ne l'ai jamais connu ; mais, parce que je connais son nom, son nom me connaît.
En fait, tout ce que je savais, c'était qu'il avait dit : je suis Jésus.

Ainsi, peut-être que c'est son nom secret.
C'était une belle journée ; une journée trop belle pour la tristesse, le malheur ; même si nous avons quitté l'heure du bonheur sur la terre. Un malheur qui ne sait pas, mais qui voit — qui voit qu'il n'y a rien à voir. Qui sait que tout ce qu'il y a à savoir, c'est le néant.

Un néant qui ne peut être vu sans terre.

Où peut-être « lui » seul sait où.

Le temps était magnifique, et les nuages ont appelé à l'esprit le vaisseau de l'Odyssée. Peut-être, une chanson apte au temps. Je n'ai pas senti un instant que je devais être dans ce vaisseau — c'était peut-être la chanson. Après tout, il ne faut pas oublier que le temps vient du temps — mais peut-être seulement dans une chanson, dans toutes les chansons. Et que les chansons sont dangereuses surtout lorsque vous écoutez leur appel — elles apportent le malheur.

Surtout lorsqu'on essaie de retourner à la terre.

Surtout lorsqu'on peut voir la terre.

Mais maintenant, « il » était déjà terre — une terre qui se passait dans la mer.

Viens, viens, venez.
Je n'étais pas sûr si c'était une voix, ou une chanson — ou d'où ça venait. Peut-être, c'était seulement dans ma tête. Mais, nous avons déjà dit : toutes les chansons sont déjà — quelquefois — dangereuses.

Mais, peut-être seulement si quelqu'un entend la chanson — et est-ce même une chanson si personne ne l'entend? Toutefois, entendre quelque chose ne signifie pas que l'on comprend son sens — ou sait d'où il est venu.

L'écoute de l'appel — mais, de quelque chose d'inconnu.

Et, puisque nous ne savons pas d'où vient la chanson, je la nomme : chanson de la mer.

Une chanson avec les mots « au revoir grand-père ».

***

Perhaps also
already written onto — into — one.
Quite possibly from a writing pen,
a scribendo calamus.

But then again, perhaps just into, onto, me:
after all, that is the risk of thinking, of thought — let alone of writing out one's thoughts. For, it might well been impossible to differentiate, to know, whether the thought was writing itself into one, or if it had emerged from, had always already been in, one.

In that one might well be one's own pen;
that it is one that pertains to a pen,

— *calamarius* —
where one is one's own *calamari.*

Writing oneself
as one is perhaps written upon.

Where writing might well be an inscription from another — inked into one, burned into one, *enkaustos*, marking one, where one is marked by something that burns, is caustic, combustible even, *kaustos.* And, not just the other that is in front of one, that is somewhat present to one, but the other that is absent, is named as other, is absent as (s)he, it, is named as other.

But nonetheless, still made by one.
Perhaps in memory of a name.

But, of course, the moment we do, the moment we inscribe, we are also attempting to lock down in time, perhaps pause time, rupture time: capture — lock up — in time.

Enframe
in
a
cenotaph.

... fear of death was perhaps the root of all art, perhaps also of all things of the mind. We fear death, we shudder at life's instability, we grieve to see the flowers wilt again, and again, and the leaves fall, and in our hearts we know that we, too, are transitory and will soon disappear. When artists create pictures and thinkers search for laws and formulate thoughts, it is in order to salvage

Where what is written, penned down, is perhaps also pinned down: not just because all writing is the inscription of a version — keeping in mind that one can only write what one knows, a particular memory, what one recalls — but that,

something from the great dance of death, to make something that lasts longer than we do.

— Hermann Hesse

since forgetting potentially haunts every memory, not only is each particular possibly peculiar, one's own (*peculiaris*) — where it might wander away from the flock (*pecu*, cattle) — each moment of writing might well be a setting in place, a remembering, of a forgotten, a what was *not-there*.

Not in the sense of an absence; but a *not-yet* and *was-always-already*, at the same time.

So, not that one is inscribing what is dead — for, each remembrance might well be a resurrection, where one is *doing this in memory of me* — but that each scripting is a moment when one is quite possibly writing death.

Thus, always also — and here one cannot quite know if we are hearing a false echo or not — quite possibly a calamity, *calamitatem*. Where perhaps — since death, even whilst it is being written, is the unknowability that haunts whilst remaining unknown — writing cannot know of itself even whilst writing.

Perhaps even betrays itself — as writing — whilst writing.

Not just because we write, one writes.

But quite possibility because of writing — of what is betrayed by writing itself. For, as Blanchot writes, « what is betrayed by writing is not what writing would have to transcribe and that could not be *trans*cribed, it is writing itself, which betrayed, appeals to laughter, to tears, to passive impassiveness, seeking to write more passively than any passivity ».[9]

So perhaps then, writing as
an encounter of death with death —
l'instant de ma mort.

Which is not to say that the one who writes isn't involved, implicated, in an encounter of death, with death, of death with death, in the instant of writing itself. For, as Avi teaches us in *Dictations*, the one who takes down, who opens her ear to writing, the secretary, scrivener, is as much the writer as the one dictating: for, the scribe is the one leaving the inscription as (s)he is inscribing, leaving her mark as (s)he marks, leaving her hand in the writing — perhaps even, hers is the mark that remains.

Which opens, or perhaps leaves us with, the question: *does one choose what one writes*, or *does it come to one?* A question that might well remain a question: for, it is not as if one can ever know — at least for sure — whether one is responding to something, or if it is a response only because one is responding. So, *a question which might well remain a quest that remains.*

Which remains *avant la lettre.*

Perhaps not just that the quest remains in the question, but that the question is also what remains of the quest. A supplementary relation: but where one cannot quite say, know, discern, neither the limit nor the necessary condition — just that both are in a relationality with, are perhaps both with, in, within, each other.

Before the letter: not just before the ink dries, but perhaps before the ink is even on the paper.

Still — moving — ink.

Where perhaps the difference between stillness and movement is the cut, the *caesura* — a separation which links, breaks whilst joining.

Touches.

The point of reading itself.

Where perhaps the only difference is the moment at which, the time in which, one sees; where, when, in which, one thinks one sees. Perhaps then, the moment of reading is nothing other than the time of the squirt, the time when the ink squirts.

Which is also the question of timing; bringing with it the dossier of the relationality between time, reading, writing, and the text; perhaps even the question of *what is the time of a, the, text?*

And when does one — can one — know if it is the text which calls out? And even if it does, is it us — is it one — whom it is calling out to?

Or perhaps, *how does one listen out for, listen to, a text if one doesn't quite know whether the call is even for one? If one is only eavesdropping?*

Keeping in mind that the difference between hearing and listening might well be a cut: that one only listens when one ceases hearing, ceases to hear.

Perhaps here, at the risk of turning to, tuning into, tuning ourselves into, an erroneous frequency, we might listen in to, into, Michel Foucault's talk, to Foucault speaking with Claude Bonnefoy, in an conversation that has since been called, entitled — perhaps by Bonnefoy, perhaps by Phillipe Artières, perhaps in, during, by, a conversation between the two — *Le beau danger*, the beautiful danger; then translated, *traduit en anglais*, by Robert Bononno, as *Speech Begins after Death*. Two rather different titles. And, if one were being pedantic, one could even accuse Bononno of being unfaithful, an infidel — but at the same time, perhaps always already more faithful. For, this is phrase which Bononno takes, one could say pilfers, from within the text — or perhaps, one could say that he allows Foucault to echo both within and without, allows him to frame his own text. In Foucault's words — words heard by, which we hear through, Bonnefoy, that we read through, which are inscribed by Bonnono — « for me, speech begins after death and once that break has been established ».[11]

For we should try to not forget that, whilst translating, *lors de la traduction*, the one who is doing so is leading, guiding (*ducere*), thus always making a decision, a choice, whilst never quite being certain, whilst unable to be sure, if (s)he is translating faithfully, moving the bones of the saint to the right place or not.

And perhaps here, we should try not to forget to attend to the oft forgotten, to the background, the less seen, to the subtitle — *entretien avec Claude Bonnefoy*, in conversation with Claude Bonnefoy — a subtitle that remains the same, insofar as two languages can ever be the same, even with a different title. A subtitle which opens the possibility that it is precisely *l'entretien*, the conversation, the speaking with, that is the danger, the beautiful danger; a danger that could only happen after death, that could only begin to be beautiful because of death.

Speaking with — a beautiful death.

Car, quand je t'interroge est-ce pour te donner la parole, ou pour te la prendre?[12]

For, when I question you is it to give you the gift of speech, or to take it from you?

In speaking with you, with another, by attending to the speech of another, does one have to inevitably listen, *écouter*, *couper*, cut.

After all, every moment of choice, every moment one chooses, every response to a particular call might be nothing other than one tuning oneself, attuning oneself, to the call of the sirens.

Thus, always already, a certain act of faith.

One which Foucault speaks about — if one were feeling a tad cheeky, one could say — confesses: « one day in Madrid, I had been fascinated by Velàzquez's *Las Meninas*. I'd been looking at the painting for a long time, just like that, without thinking about talking about it someday, much less of describing it — which at the time would have seemed derisive and ridiculous. And then one day, I don't recall how, without having looked at it since, without even having looked at a reproduction, I had this urge to write about the painting from memory, to describe what was in it. As soon as I tried to describe it, a certain colouration of language, a certain rhythm, a certain form of analysis, especially, gave me the impression, the near certainty — false, perhaps — that I had found exactly the right language by which the distance between ourselves and classical philosophy of representation and the classical ideas of orders and resemblance could come into focus and be evaluated. That's how I began to write *The Order of Things* ».[13]

A call not just of memory, but from a memory of what could well have not been the thing itself: perhaps that is the very condition of the order of things. Or even, that *is* the order of things; not just *les mots et les choses*, but *les mots avant les choses.*

Which is not to say that words and things are necessarily separate. For, one should try to not forget that words matter, should attempt to never forget the materiality of words, perhaps even of thought — insofar as an idea is translated, led, perhaps even betrayed, into language; where to Socrates' chagrin *eikos* and *eidos* might well be somewhat indistinguishable; a worry, a warning, about representation that could only come about through writing, representation — faithfulness to a teaching, his teacher's teaching, through an act of, through Plato's act of, infidelity.

Perhaps then words — that we hear, see, read — are traces

of this infidelity to thought, marks of a thought of infidelity; remains of a thought bringing itself before us, presenting itself to us. Or perhaps, it is only one that thinks that it is before one — one that calls, is calling, what is before us thought; speaking for it as thought, as if it is thought. Thus, not just words standing in for thought, in place of thought, but that the one who reads, sees, hears, is *speaking for*, speaking in place of, what (s)he is attempting to respond to, respond with.

Prosopopoeia.

Where reading is perhaps an animation of, where reading is animating, thought.

Necromancy.

A reanimation that might well be a desecration, an act of complete infidelity — but one born of an attempt to respond to, with; absolute fidelity.

Which might be why — just as we were about to walk out of the forest in Saas Fee — as I was asking Avi how to respond to a block in writing, to deal with the dreaded *writer's block*, she turned to me and said, « perhaps you need to move your books around … »

Animate them to learn from them (*boccræft*, book learning), to open them, to open oneself to learning from them, being literate to them. Whilst never forgetting that even as one might have been the one who has taken the books — off a shelf, from the bookstore, a library, from the interwebs — and laid them on one's desk, bed, table, one's reasons for doing so, and the those of the books themselves, might not quite be the same: particularly if the register of sequence, relationality, order of things, of words, *les choses avant les mots, ou même les choses sont les mots*, is opened.

Thus, even as animation might be taking place, who is animating what — or what is animating whom — remains a question that is quite possibly beyond one.

Perhaps always already — to return to Avi's teaching — an act in which « one has to trust oneself » ; perhaps always already a relationality of trust between one and one's books.

For, even our great archivist Foucault teaches us, « for [*Les mots et les choses*] I used material I had gathered in the preceding years almost at random, without knowing what I would do with it, with no certainty about the possibility of ever writing an essay. In a way it was like examining a kind of inert material, an abandoned garden of some sort, an unusable expanse, which I surveyed the way I imagined the sculptor of old, the sculptor of the seventeenth or eighteenth century, might contemplate, might touch the block of marble he didn't yet know what to do with ».[14]

Or, as sculptor, teacher, LaSallean brother, Joseph McNally
constantly teaches,
the work emerges from the material.

Foucault continues, in a line, sentence, speech, from before

— after all, this is me reading Bonnefoy writing, transcribing, being the scrivener to his conversation with Foucault — « … in one sense my head is empty when I begin to write, even though my mind is always directed towards a specific object ».[15]

My mind. *Mon esprit. L'esprit.* Spirit.

Perhaps then also: *my mind is always being directed towards a specific object.*

Where writing, my writing, the moment when I write, is an attempt to listen to this directing, this guiding. After all, « for me » — for Foucault, but also for me — « writing is an extremely gentle activity, hushed. I get the impression of velvet when I write ».[16]

« Ultimately, I don't write because I have something in mind, I don't write to show what I have already demonstrated and analyzed for myself. Writing consists essentially of doing something that allows me to discover something I hadn't seen initially. When I begin to write an essay or a book, or anything, I don't really know where it's going to lead or where it'll end up or what I'm going to show. I only discover what I have to show in the actual movement of writing, as if writing specifically meant diagnosing what I had wanted to say at the very moment I begin to write ».[17]

« I don't know.
In any event, it involves an activity of language
that is extremely profound for me ».[18]

Where there is no writer, only writing.

Where, « for me, writing is a wandering after death and not a path to the source of life. It is in this sense that my language is profoundly anti-Christian, probably more so than the themes I continue to evoke ».[19]

Which might be why,
« for me », — for you, Michel, and for me —
« writing is an extremely gentle activity, hushed.
I get the impression of velvet when I write ... »[20]

With the soundless sound of a pen sliding — walking — across paper, fingers tapping — treading — on, over, a keyboard; « throughout which all kinds of inaudible voices seemed to sound and echo and all sorts of visible-invisible figures roamed. Music out of the primeval world, from whence I cannot tell, stole on my ear ».[21] Where perhaps the one writing, the scrivener, me, we, are doing nothing but attempting to inscribe the unheard, unhearable — the silent sound of the moving, the movement, of ink.

Where, to echo Hélène Cixous, my teacher's — one of Avi's — teachers, one of my favourite writers speaking, writing, about writing, about her writing, about how she writes: « ... quickly and without a sound I pick up the pad that doesn't leave my bedside and the large-nibbed pen with which you can write big and quickly across the paper, and I noted the first lines the Coming dictated to me, filling in the darkness the great page at tremendous speed with these inestimable phrases, leaven of the book, gift of the gods whose name I don't even know ... »[22]

Squirt.

Où, ce n'est pas un calmar.

But perhaps — always already ink.

... isn't every
letter a love letter?
... What I didn't
know
was
that by
writing
love
letters,
I was
writing
letters
to love.

— *Chris Kraus*

... writing letters,
however, means to
denude oneself
before the ghosts,
something for
which they greedily
wait. Written kisses
don't reach their
destination, rather
they are drunk on
the way by the
ghosts ...

— Franz Kafka

LOVE LETTERS

LOVE LETTERS

What would that make a word, every word, then?
Perhaps a collection, a coming together, a site, space, of — for — love.

Le mot.
L'amour.

Awaiting reception. Awaiting landing. For, every letter is already sent, sent off — the moment it is written, it has already left one; it has already been committed to, become, language; put into letters. Thus, ever letter is always already *après la lettre*. Or, perhaps even only becomes a letter at the moment of the letter, becomes a letter during its writing; where its becoming is inseparable from its lettering. Which means that it is only a letter at the point where it is seen, read, as one; the moment it lands.

Where it ends up is another question entirely; as is where it lands. Questions that can only be addressed either retrospectively, or if one attaches it to a definite frame of time, if one frames the question in and through a finite period.

And even then, that would only be a locating, a location of, the letter at a particular moment in time, at that moment in which it is located; a moment that is perhaps only a *caesura* in its flight. Thus, one can never quite be certain if the letter was going to, just about to, move on, continue, keep moving. Not that one would ever be able to tell if a letter that seems to have landed has only stopped momentarily, taken a little rest. Perhaps any attempt to speak of the locus of a letter is one that might be a little too soon, a little premature, potentially too early, before; always possibly *avant la lettre*.

Moreover, since words can be composed of, could be made up of, more than one letter, this suggests there might always also be multiple missives …

The word is only the witness who saw what happened.

Is the very conception of a word then always already a fixing in place — no matter how momentary — of a word?

In homage — perhaps even in fidelity — to Yves Klein. Who, in my mind, said: « the painting is only the witness who saw what happened » ; a line that I first heard from, through, Giorgio Agamben during his seminar at the European Graduate School in August 2004. Perhaps it was apt that I first heard this — a line that has left its mark on, in, me, even as, perhaps precisely because, I have never been able to verify its source, origin, *auctor*, author — in a seminar entitled *Homo Sacer*. After all, one is often-times moved beyond oneself by something from beyond, something unknown, unknowable — something that the profane is unable to understand, something sacred; not necessarily divine, but something that maintains its secret.

Where the word testifies through itself, its site — where the word is a gravestone: marking the absence of a letter that has already gone, been sent, flown away.

Le mot.
L'amour.
La mort.

It has taken me years to admit — perhaps only to myself — that I don't care about writing something important, something significant. That my only hope, wish — dream even — is to write something beautiful.

Every love letter
is
love to letters …

— Wong May Ee

*The arteries of
the hand & arm
that write lead
straight into
the heart …*

— Chris Kraus

So in a sense love is just like writing: living in such a heightened state that accuracy and awareness are vital.

— Chris Kraus

And, if love and writing are potentially in a relationality with each other, are quite possibly resounding with each other, the echoes of Roland Barthes' teaching that « language is a skin: I rub my language against the other. It is as if I had words instead of fingers, or fingers at the tip of my words »[2] is never far away from us.

Which opens the question — even as one thinks, believes, that one is on the same wavelength as the other whom one is writing to, quite possibly in love with — *are we in tune*?

Can we ever be in tune?
Or, are we only ever in tune with? Thus, always already a relation, in relation — where being in tune is not just with another, but premised on there being an other.

Thus, also a touching.
Where being in tune is a touch. Fingers, words, sounds.
Keeping in mind Jean-Luc Nancy's reminder that « it is space that one needs to even begin to touch. » So, even as there are two or more in relation — in a relationality — what one is in tune with is a *space between.*

Attempting to listen to that space, to *what is not.*
Where being attuned — where the tune — lies in the *not-*.
Where the dash is precisely the space needed; never forgetting that even as it connects, it can also break.
Be dashed.

Perhaps potentially detune one's self as one attempts to tune into another.

And here, we should try to remember — keeping in mind that memory is of the order of calling back, perhaps calling forth, certainly a calling, recalling, a touching of the past into the present — that citation is an attempt to resound with the voice of another.

Not just in the form of a homage, but also an enactment of violence to the other, on another. A touching that potentially wounds. That not only echoes another, but perhaps always also steals, takes over, away, her voice.

Prosopopoeia.

Hence an attuning, attunement, that always already detunes both the self, one, and the other that one is attempting to be in tune with.

A tuning that is a relationality that potentially undoes all tuning.

A *détunenement*, if you will.

And yet, both are also already in tune with each other.

A tune that can be felt by those in the relationality. However, since they are both detuned, this suggests that this is a tune that lies outside the boundaries of knowability.

And if potentially beyond cognition, this also suggests that it is a tune that comes to them from elsewhere.

A tune that tunes them; that perhaps moves them in a manner that remains unknown to them.

Auto-tune.

And since this is something that is beyond us, perhaps the only thing that we, one, can say, that is left for one to say is — allowing the irony that I have borrowed the voice of another to say it to resound —

Perhaps then, I will have to show you …

… nothing I tell you will enlighten you. I await the poetical expression of what I have to say.

— Jean Genet

… bearing in mind the potential impossibility of seeing a tune; even if the effects of the said tune, song, might well be visible. After all, it is not as if relationality has a presence; even if it might be ever-present, even if it might be a strong presence between the two (or more) involved, even if there might not be the very notion of two — of a *we* — without the relation itself.

Perhaps then, even as writing on, about, is quite possibly an act of love, it might well be a gesture of sending forth.

Where what is sent out is not just a relation of love — a statement, posting, post-card which is a nod towards the love for the other, the object that one is writing about — but that the very object is brought forth in the writing itself.

Even if it is a *love song for a city* …

… a title that I could not quite decide on, even as I have already decided, declared, named even: a title that is always already haunted by the question 'should it have been a love song *to* rather than *for* a city?' For, if *for*, does it, does one, already assume, presume, to know, to know this city, to know what a city is, to know that there even is a city — to know you.

It should have been easier to speak of, write about, you — to say who you are. After all, I've been here for quite some time, quite a while. Thirty-three years to be exact: a number that might even be seen to be quite significant in some places, cultures, traditions. But perhaps, only significant — its signification might always remain, be, beyond one, beyond me.

Even as — perhaps especially when — one attempts to write on, speak of, it.

And here, it might be appropriate recall the lesson that Jacques Derrida never lets us forget: in love, there is an impossible tension — a tension of the impossible — between the *who* and the *what*. Do we love someone, something, for what she is — her characteristics — or who (s)he is, the person, the thing, as such? For, if one loves another for what (s)he is, these characteristics can change, fade away, alter, disappear. More importantly, these very characteristics can be found elsewhere, in others — and thus, there is a flattening, no matter how slight, of the person, all persons, into the same. In order to maintain the singularity of another, (s)he has to remain wholly other from oneself — thus, (s)he always remains at least partially veiled from one, retains a certain unknowability, lingers outside of our comprehension,

prehension, grasp. However, even as one attempts to respond to the *who* of another, it is not as if one can ever even glimpse *who* (s)he is without the *what*; it is not as if one can ever completely separate what (s)he is from who (s)he is.

And more than that, since it is only the *what* that is potentially apparent to one, one might never quite know exactly *who* one is attempting to respond to, with. Not just because the *who* might remain hidden from one, but that the *what* might always already be haunted by spectres of the *who*.

And when one speaks of hauntings, when one opens the dossier of haunts, one should try not to forget that we call places, spaces that we are familiar with, comfortable in, our haunts as well. Places where our memories are born, that flood back to us when we recall them — their spaces, times, peoples. Places that continue to haunt our thoughts, our lives. Though, the moment one speaks of memories, of remembering, one should also bear in mind that one has no control over what one forgets, over forgetting itself — for, it happens to one. Thus, one can never quite know if every moment of memory is haunted by forgetting, if forgetting is part of memory itself. Thus, our haunts — even our most treasured, beloved, ones — are always already haunted by, haunted with, the possibility of never quite being ours.

And here, at least momentarily, we should open our receptors to an Austrian voice, to a Viennese accent, to one Sigmund Freud and his warning of the *unheimlich*: the uncanny, the *unhomely*. To a certain unfamiliarity with the familiar; to a certain — for we are beyond the pale of certainty here — uneasiness, weirdness even, of an unknowability within what, in whatever, one thinks one knows.

Which opens the question of — keeping in mind the echoes of quests, journeys, movement, in all questions — *how does one speak of a space, a place?*

Particularly, if one calls it one's home?

For, when speaking of it, it is not just that one is attempting to read it, interpret it (momentarily leaving aside the problems of separating hermeneutics from Hermes, from divine promises), but that one might well be writing, re-writing, this home, this city, into being. For, writing — *écriture* — always already quite possibly brings with it echoes of a *cri*, a cry. Or even — as Nietzsche reminds us — a scream, *schreien*, in each act, every moment, of *schreiben*, writing. After all, writing itself — scribbles, *scribere* — invokes openings, tearings; and if it happens to move us, or even wound us, perhaps a certain tearing as well.

Causes us to fall.

Just like, love.

And here, if one thinks that I am being a tad dramatic, one should try not to forget that the city, the old city, the ancient city, was called, comes from the term *civitas*, (in which we hear notions of citizenship, membership in the community, and later on state, commonwealth, and so forth). In it, one can hear echoes of *civis* (townsman), drawn from the Proto Indo-European **kei-* (to lie, rest) in which resounds the Greek *keimai* (I lie down), from which we have *koiman* (to put to sleep), *koimeterion* (sleeping place), *coemeterium*, cemetery. So, even as cities are continually, perhaps even quite desperately, attempting to move, remove, death from their midst, one should open one's receptors to its ghosts which might, perhaps can, never be fully exorcised.

But even as we tune our receptors to the potential death in all cities, a city, our city, one should try not to forget that **kei-* also brings with it another sense, that of *beloved, dear*. After all, we only lay to rest the ones we love. More importantly, the ones we love are the ones that lie with one even after one has laid them to rest, after one thinks one has laid them to rest. And one's love for them, even if a love that one cannot understand — for, we have to keep in mind that love comes from elsewhere, strikes one, takes one from behind, as it were — is dear to one, costs one, especially when one holds it dearly, when it is dear to one.

Thus, the ones that one loves — along with one's love for them, for another, others, the others — continue to haunt one. But, this might well be a haunting that is not unwelcomed, perhaps even is a haunting that haunts in a manner that feels homely to one. So, even as it is an unfamiliarity with the familiar, there is always also a familiarity with the unfamiliar.

Perhaps this is why *home is where the heart it*. Not due to some banal romantic idealisation, but because it is a haunt that continues haunting, that it is one's haunt — in that one finds comfort in it, in there, in the place, in its space — even as it haunts one with, even as one is haunted by, the fact that it might always slip away, like a ghost, a spectre, that it might always already have disappeared, and be nothing other than a memory about to be forgotten.

Perhaps then, in a strange roundabout way, this is an opening gesture, my gesture towards an opening — I should take responsibility for it — to an acknowledgment of a relationality to the city, to the home; a recognition that all that I can say about the city, all thoughts about her that might come to me, thoughts that are to come, are little songs, attempts to tune in to, attune myself to, the space, place, to her, whilst never being able to be sure of all that I see, never knowing if I am only seeing blindly.

But perhaps always: with — in — fidelity.

To nothing other than the possibility of a city, to the possibility that is called a city, to the possibility that I have named her: a — perhaps even my — city.[4]

Perhaps only my city insofar as (s)he is a city which has claimed me — in which I have been named a citizen; where I have been designated, designed, tasked even, to sleep, to rest, to lay myself down.

"My"—what does this word designate? Not what belongs to me, but what I belong to, what contains my whole being, which is mine insofar as I belong to it.

— Søren Kierkegaard

Where perhaps — as Jean Genet might say — in talking about a city, « I'm not talking about a dead cemetery, but about a living one … »

Where, it is dead to me: precisely because someone can only be dear to me when it is residing in me, within me, when it is mine to recall, remember.

A living dead.

Perhaps then, not so much *killing yourself to live* — as Black Sabbath might have it — but that for something to live in you, the very first thing you would have to do is to kill it. But, then again, if someone is only « mine insofar as I belong to it », it may well be that the act of preservation, of keeping it as one's own, is first and foremost an act of suicide.

Keeping in mind here — allowing the irony of doing so to resound — that « life does not have, here or there, its own proper(ty), its own literalness; life produces itself as the circle of its own reappropriation, the self-return before which there is no proper self ». Thus, it can only be known, recognised as it were, the second time it is seen. However, seeing as *life is movement*, is ever-changing, this suggests that there can be — there is the distinct possibility that there is — no second time; at least, none that can be known. Or, as Derrida continues, « nothing precedes the return ... » : which might well be not just the fact that there is no thing (that can be known) before the return, but that is it is precisely nothing that comes just before the return; that the return of something — the thing that allows us to catch a glimpse of knowability — is always preceded by nothing. Or, perhaps even: that something always already brings with it nothing; a nothing that continues to haunt it, make its home within it, that we might well mistake the haunting for familiarity.

Which might well make all attempts to describe it — even this one, perhaps particularly this one — completely futile.

Which might also be what leads Elfriede Jelinek to proclaim: « language is worth as little as life itself, for it is life itself ».[8] In, and through, language no less: but it is not as if she didn't already know that. More importantly perhaps, not only might there have been no other way in which she could have made that statement, it would only make sense — allowing the possibility that sense and nonsense might not quite be separable here — within language itself.

er nicht als er

A reflection on Robert Walser that could only have come — not through his name but — through the sound of his name itself. Where perhaps it is only a sound that remains after his proper name, as it were, has gone for a walk, *auf einen spaziergang*.

A reflection on Robert Walser in which he is always already absent: never there. Where there is speech: but neither by him, nor even about him — at least not directly. Where there is a conversation — « *a number of people to each other, all very friendly and well-behaved (perhaps lying in bathtubs as was once the custom in mental hospitals)* »[9] — but in which the one who reads never quite knows who is speaking, if there are even multiple people speaking, if they are all *perhaps* speaking at the same time; and — in the absence of any diacritical marks indicating speech — if there even is anyone who speaks.

But perhaps, this might be the only way in which one can speak about a writer, about one who writes: for, as Jelinek points out, or has one of her characters say — not that we can ever differentiate the two —, « the writer goes forth from himself and then right away goes right away from himself, old and decrepit; he can only bring someone else to life, never revive himself ».[10]

Where perhaps the writer can never quite write "I"; at least not in the sense of a mark that refers to herself: thus, perhaps always only an "I" that remains within quotation marks, within vampire marks that suck all the life out of the "I"; where the "I" that remains is one preyed upon by the one without reflection.

Where all the "I" does is reflect that it cannot reflect anything other than the mark itself.

Where perhaps it shows nothing other than what it shows: and where all the one who reads does — all one can do — is to attempt to listen, to catch a whisper of what it no longer reflects.

Now who does the writer mean by himself?

— Elfriede Jelinek

To listen —
to open oneself to the possibility of another,
the potentiality of being in communication with another;
an other that might be completely other not just to one, but to itself.
Where the otherness of another is perhaps what keeps this communion from being a consumption;
even as both are attempting to touch.

To speak;
is to converse, to be in conversation.
Bearing in mind that to converse is to live with, to turn about (*vertere*) with (*con*). But, not necessarily in agreement: for, to converse is also to be the exact opposite. Which means: to converse is to be with whilst also possibly turning around (*conversus*), turning about (*convertere*). But, even in, even when there is, disagreement it is an opposition that continues to maintain the relation; that still agrees to be with. That even in divergence, even as one is momentarily turned away from or even against (*versus*) the other, there is always already an openness to the possibility of changing one's mind, one's position, an openness to the possibility of conversion.

You can always focus on musicality but it won't help. Music is always a stranger on this earth, but the disadvantage of language is that it can all too quickly seem familiar and so you throw it off, horrified, as though you'd touched something disgusting.

— Elfriede Jelinek

Where « speaking is when silence at last falls silent ».[11]

And where reading — attempting to read — is nothing other than an attempt to respond to this silent silence.

Perhaps then, not just *blind reading*, or that one is *reading blindly* — and that the very blindness in, within, reading itself is not just structural — but that one can only catch a glimpse of this blindness, one's own blindness, not by seeing it (for, that would undo the very notion of blindness itself — which does not mean that this is not, does not remain, a possibility) but by hearing its whisper.

Allowing all the absurdity — perhaps even impossibility — of seeing sound to resound here. But, then again, who ever said that reading was confined to sight. Or that, sound could not open oneself to the possibility of seeing; even if what one is looking at cannot quite be seen.

Which perhaps opens the question: what is the sound in a love letter, of a love letter.

Which might well be the question: *what is the sound of love?*

Which is also the question of: can you hear, recognise, know, how love sounds?

Trying not to forget that if love is an openness to the possibility of another, it is singular; and, hence, each time it occurs, takes place, is always already both the first and the last time. Thus, there is no data — or, quite possibly, even known date — of love: perhaps only a *datum*, insofar as Dora remains all-giving and always also already unknowable. For, one should bear in mind that the moment the one who was all-gifted attempts to open the jar, the moment Pandora attempts to discover, find out, comprehend, grasp, what is within that which she is gifted, is also the moment when all hell breaks loose. And perhaps, if one is being playful, one could speculate that there is only hope as she closed the lid on it, trapping it — where hope lies precisely in its being unseen, unknown …

… an object.

You don't remember the quiet moments. You remember fights. You remember seeing the girl kissing another guy at a party, or you remember a moment where you took ecstasy with a girl and you're on the beach all night long — small images. But the truth is that the most lovingful moments are quite hard to remember. Because they're musical. They're not narrative. The moments of hugging and kissing or making love, they're usually colored abstract or emotional.

— Gaspar Noé

I memorize
every line
And I kiss the
name that you
sign
And darling,
then I read
again right
from the start
Love letters
straight from
your heart

— Edward Heyman
& Victor Young

You should
never have
agreed to be a
god for me if
you were afraid
to assume the
duties of a
god, and we
all know that
they are not as
tender as all
that. You have
already seen
me cry. Now
you must learn
to relish my
tears.

OBJECTIFY ME PLEASE ...

OBJECTIFY ME PLEASE ...

One of the recurring tropes, conceits, of modern society is that we want to be unique, different from anyone else. Even if we ignore the fact that any notion of difference requires comparison, the problem is: if we were completely different from every other, there would not be any society in the first place. The very status of our selves in, and as, a society rests — quite possibly relies — on similarity.

In itself, this would not be a problem. But, if we consider the fact that being a hermit isn't quite the life-style for most of us, one has then to deal with the paradoxical situation of wanting to be individual and wanting to be like others at the same time. This is, of course, the hinge around which the capitalist enterprise functions: *buy my product so you can be like everyone else who wants to be an individual.* And, unless one is a froth-at-the-mouth Marxist, one will probably not have any issue acknowledging the fact that most of us are basically fine living within this paradoxical paradigm. For, this only suggests that we are not logical beings.

However, to merely dismiss it at this juncture would completely miss the point.

Since we are approaching a non-logical situation, we have to consider why it still continues to haunt us. After all, it is not as if questions of identity have disappeared: in many ways as modern society develops, the question of "who am I?" appears with increasing frequency. And if we posit that "who am I?" is both a result and the cause of the paradox we face (for, without the question, the notion of the individual and one's relation to society would not even exist) this suggests that it resides in the realm of the imaginary.

Perhaps then, to begin to address the paradox, we have to first attempt to address the question itself. For, one cannot ignore the fact that "who am I?" lies in the realm of hermeneutics; even if it is not limited to it. Thus, it can also take the form of *what is the meaning of my life?* Which is a question of significance, of importance — of what something, or someone, means to you — rather than that of semantics, of signification. In other words, it is an attempt to discover *how important am I to others.* Hence, the notion of "I" is always already intrinsically linked to others: in fact, even as alterity, otherness, may be its limit, the other is the very condition of the possibility of "I" itself.

Thus, not only is *self and another* not antonymous, both are always already a part of each other, even as they are quite possibly always also somewhat apart. Or, as Jean-Luc Nancy might say, the self is *singular-plural*; and without others, the "I" means nothing.

And here, we should keep in mind that the only thing that can be simultaneously individual and part of a collective — itself and also part of a series of other things — is an object. Where, perhaps within our obsession with discovering "who am I?" lies a secret fantasy: that of being objectified.

And, whenever the dossier of *object* is opened, registers of acquisition, possession, ownership, come with it; notions that are quite possibly objected to. But here, it might be helpful to remind ourselves, once again, of Kierkegaard's reminder that « my » designates « not what belongs to me, but what I belong to, what contains my whole being, which is mine insofar as I belong to it ».[1] That one can only have an object insofar as one also belongs to it. And it is this duality that remains crucial to us. For, even as there is a constant duel between the "I" and all others, one must never forget that it takes two to duel: without the duality there is nothing at all.

Perhaps though, what remains secret is the precise relation of this duo. "Who am I?" is imaginary as what is being imagined is the "I" itself. For, even as we are in a system of objects, one should try to not forget that there is a part of us — a *who*, as it were — that remains unknown in the *what*.

It is impossible that we should each survive the other. That's the duel, the axiomatic of every duel, the scene which is the most common and the least spoken of — or the most prohibited — concerning our relation to the other. Yet the impossible happens — not in 'objective reality', which has no say here, but in the experience of Romeo and Juliet. And under the law of the pledge, which commands every given word.

— Jacques Derrida

And this is the very juncture of love.

For, even as love is an openness to another, another that remains wholly her or him self, there has to be a moment when one can also say that the other is yours. This is the very violence inherent in love: when one utters "I love you" one is selecting an other from every other. And it is this that Marilyn Manson captures perfectly through his phrase, « I can't sleep till I devour you »[2]. More than that, one is inflicting this selection regardless of the will of the other person: for, each utterance happens at a singular moment, one where one has, can have, no idea how the other feels. Perhaps then, always already a moment of terror: an imposition of the self not just on, but perhaps even over, the other. Where, at the moment of the utterance, the other remains a complete enigma.

***

Plato teaches us that the perfect relationship between two persons can be found in *philia*. In an ideal world, there would be *agape* but since we are not of the order of the divine, that is quite possibly always already beyond us. *Eros*, whilst exciting and enticing, is excessive; a reasonable, rational, person would protect herself from such extremes. And thus, a good friendship is measured, controlled, where both parties remain fully in, and of, themselves: and since the good and the beautiful go hand in hand, a proper friendship is also beautiful.

For, when there is proper balance, the two parties in that relationality remain fully singular. In other words, their very *self* is secure.

And it is this very security that is brought into question by Heinrich von Kleist in his essay 'On the Marionette Theatre'. For, when beauty, or « grace is concerned, it is impossible for man to come anywhere near a puppet ». The implication of which is that one has to be an object to be graceful; for, it is « consciousness [that] can disturb natural grace » ; a notion that is addressed in a tale about a boy who fall is caused by « vanity », awareness of his own self; the same fate that we face, « now that we've eaten of the tree of knowledge ». And, it is our knowledge of *good* and *evil* and more importantly of ourselves — shame, awareness of their own nakedness, was the first thing that struck woman and man after eating of the tree — that prevents one from being graceful, that distances one from « free play ». And, it is only « as thought grows dimmer and weaker [that] grace emerges more brilliantly and decisively ».

But, it is not as if it is completely beyond us.

For, « grace itself returns when knowledge has as it were gone through an infinity. Grace appears most purely in that human form which either has no consciousness or an infinite consciousness. That is, in the puppet on in the ». Where, in terms of grace, « only a god can equal inanimate matter in this respect ».

Hence, it is not so much that the human — one that is *anima* — is unable to be graceful; it is the fact that the human is too aware of her own humanness, of his own self. And it is this which prevents the « soul » from becoming a « line » : a *line* being « nothing other than the path taken by the soul of the dancer ». Where self-consciousness, or « affectation », is the point when the « soul, or moving force, appears at some point other than the centre of gravity of the movement ».

In other words, not only has the answer to Yeats' quip « can we tell the dancer from the dance? » be *no*, we have to take it even further — *there is no dancer without the dance*. Where, it is only in the moment of dance that one is potentially a dancer. And, it is perhaps only in the moment when one is immersed in the craft, *tekhnē* — dance in this case — that it can possibly elevate, be elevated — after all, one never quite knows, can perhaps never know, who or what does this elevation — into a art. And here, one should try to never forget the fact that Tekhnē herself is a *daemon*: and it is only when she whispers in one's ear that there is the possibility of art. This is an approach to art that acknowledges that part of art always lies outside the person; where it consumes the practitioner, often in ways which are exterior to one's cognitive ability. In this sense, art remains invisible to one; at best, it expresses itself through one.

In other words, art is nothing more than a gesture.

And more than that, since art always already remains potentially exterior to the person, there are no artists; there is only the possibility of the gesture.

This is perhaps why the tale had to be told by « an old friend » who, as he speaks, « took a pinch of snuff ». For, a tale of beauty — a story on grace — could only be recounted by one who was also outside of himself, by one who was momentarily out of control. And since it is impossible for one to « eat again of the tree of knowledge in order to return to the state of innocence », or at least not quite yet, it is quite possibly only through a drug that one temporarily escapes the confines of self-awareness.

But if one is always already beyond oneself in beauty, then what is — or, where lies — one's responsibility. Which is also a question of: *to whom, or what, is one responsible to in art?* Which translates to: should an artist be held accountable to any domain outside her work?

Which is a burning question dogging the careers, lives, of many who have been called artists — amongst them, one Roman Polanski.

In March 1977, Polanski was charged with a number of offenses against then minor, 13 year old, Samantha Gailey, in California. He initially pleaded not guilty, but later accepted a plea bargain where the initial charges were dropped for a guilty plea of unlawful sexual intercourse. However, upon learning that he was likely to face prison time and deportation, Polanski fled to France and, since then, has only lived and worked in countries that were unlikely to extradite him to the United States.[4]

Over the years, there have been two camps: one that wants Polanski brought to trial, as no one — no matter who — should be above the law; and another that calls for the charges to be cleared on the grounds that he is a great director and filmmaker.

And, even though both sides are making seemingly opposite claims, they are relying on the same premise: the artist is responsible to the public; that there is a correspondence between the artist and the world. And in both their statements, one can hear a strong echo of Plato's warning that art is potentially dangerous — it has the power to corrupt. For, since all learning is mimetic, the manner in which things are represented is crucial; any misrepresentation can harm an undiscerning mind, one that is unable to shield itself from it. This is particularly so if one conceives of Polanski as an artist: for, if his craft deemed to be of the highest level, his representations would seem to be so real, so true, that one is unable to differentiate the shadows from the truth. Hence, Polanski has to be held responsible: otherwise, those who admire him, and his work, might be misled. Or worse: those who attempt to learn from him — mimic his craft — might just be corrupted.

But, this is where they have completely missed the point.

For, by focusing on the accountability of Roman Polanski to the public, we have shifted the focus of thinking from art to the artist. And if we consider Plato's claim that art is the expression of craft at its highest level — where craft is elevated beyond itself — we have a situation that art is *mimesis that is not mimetic*. Hence, art comes into itself at the moment when craft is beyond craft. And since one can only learn mimetically — and what one is learning is craft — it stands to reason that one cannot learn art: whenever it happens, it happens to one. This is why Socrates posits that wisdom comes from beyond — *comes to him* from a *daemon* whispering into his ear.

Thus, there is no artist.
The person is, at best, the medium through which there is the possibility of art.

Which means: not only does one have to separate a judgment of Roman Polanski from the work of Roman Polanski, one has to go even further: one has to separate representations of Roman Polanski from his potential gestures of art. This calls for a judgement of his work outside of any criterion other than itself; a judgment which echoes Jacques Rancière and his claim that « the work … stands under its own law of production and is its own proof ».[5]

Where, one has to completely divorce Polanski's films from his very being.

But this leaves us this problem: how to judge the medium that is Roman Polanski? Can one really separate the potential rapist from the genius that produces work which slips into the realm of art?

Here, it might be helpful to re-tune to Rancière and his reminder that art is « the territory of thought that is present outside itself and identical with non-thought ».[6] So, even as the work « is its own proof » this suggests that we are never able to say whether a work is art. This might well be why Plato was so nervous about art: if thought and non-thought are identical, all the reason in the world could never help one distinguish — with any certainly — between them. Which means that art could affect you in ways that were always already beyond you. This also means that one's mind — even if one were a philosopher — might never be prepared, ready enough, to encounter, defend oneself from, art. One might even posit that the medium is the site of this « non-thought ». Which is why a work of art which is a work of « unconditional creativity is identified with an absolute passivity ».[7] And — here Rancière never lets us forget — when we say that Polanski is a genius, we should not forget « Kant's conception of genius [which] summarizes this duality. The genius is the active power of nature who sets his own creative power against any model or norm. The genius, we might say, becomes a norm for himself. But at the same time he is the one who does not know what he does and is incapable of accounting for his own activity ».[8]

This does not mean that as we celebrate Polanski's works as art, as we acknowledge his moments of genius, we should exonerate his behaviour. Nor should we do the opposite of shunning all that he has done, and might still do. Or even worse: adopt the standard liberal position of 'yes, he is a horrible person, but his work is good'. We should, instead, take the separation of the person from the work all the way to the end: and posit that Polanski's work has absolutely nothing to do with him as a person. He is a pure medium: for, at the point when the *daemon* whispers into his ear, he « does not know what he does ».

Roman Polanski is a genius at the point where Roman Polanski is no longer Roman Polanski.

Moreover, since one can never be certain of the status of something as art, it is always only a claim, a judgement; one that cannot rely on anything other than the fact that one is judging. Which means that, if we conceive of him as a person, or even an entity, we are mixing the medium with representations of that medium.

Perhaps then, the only thing one can do is to consider Roman Polanski as a pure medium, a conduit, a *no-thing in itself*. For, if art is the « territory of thought » and also « identified with an absolutely passivity », one should allow Polanski to be absolutely passive, to be one without a voice, to be *homo sacer*; bare life — completely divorced from the *polis*, from society.

Hence, the question of an artist's responsibility to society is moot. Not just that the artist is apart from everything, and everyone else, and thus, is irresponsible to anything but her work.

But that *there is no artist.*

Only a medium. Keeping in mind that a medium cannot be responsible to anything.

Not even to art.

***

To love someone is a moment of consummation in the precise sense that (s)he as to be consumed by you.
But in that moment of consumption, you are also eaten. Which is why one *falls in love*: at the point when Cupid's arrow strikes, not only is one seized by love, one quite possibly also momentarily ceases to be one.

Love: a coming together of two beings that are unknown to each other.

Separate — and together.

One insofar as part of another.

Where the very question — *who am I?* — is not only a question of one's, of our, significance to others, but is also an appeal to be chosen, to be special, even though we are every other, the same in a series of others. To be loved.

... love is much more than love: love is something before love ...

— Clarice Lispector

It is a plea to be an object.

A plea that one can hear in Geraldine Song's triptych, *Absence—Presence*, in which 3 couples are speaking with each other, speaking to each other, oftentimes in a manner where it would be difficult to tell if they were merely speaking at each other; or perhaps, merely *just speaking*.

Three conversations.
With pairs who appear to be speaking to — duos duelling

— rather than with. Even if they might well be attempting to; perhaps especially as they are trying particularly hard to.
A triptych — of cacophony, as it were.
Perhaps then,
sounds.

We're not in the same pot.
But we're still bound together.
It's difficult to be together and not be able
to — be — together — as one.[10]

You don't know what it's like
Baby you don't know what it's like
To love somebody
To love somebody
The way I love you[11]

And it opens the question of: if one listens, tries to listen, does it, does the sound — what one considers, perhaps even calls, a sound — come from what, who, one attempts to listen to, or is it a sound because one hears it, hears it as a sound.

Perhaps only because — one calls it a sound.

And perhaps here — retuning ourselves to Werner Hamacher's reminder that « the minimal condition to be able to hear something as something lies in my comprehending it neither as destined for me nor as somehow oriented toward someone else »[12] — one should try not to forget that to be loved, one has to be first named, called, the *object of one's desire.*

Which is something — allowing all echoes of things to resound here — that O understands perfectly. For, at the point in *Histoire d'O* when the realisation comes to her that « she was no longer free? », her instant, in fact her only, response is, « yes! thank God, she was no longer free ». For, in not being free, only by not being free, is she « light, a nymph on clouds, a fish in water, lost in happiness ».[13] After all, one should bear in mind that at no point is O forced to agree: she is not in a sadistic relationship; a slave she might be, but certainly no victim. Which opens the question: can one choose to lose one's freedom? For, even as O has always agreed to the situation — though a verbal contract — she also recognises that it is from an « authority outside herself ».[14] Which brings with it another question: can there be an internal authority; that is, unless one is one's own other. For, even if the register of conscience is opened, the voice inside one's head is still heard by one — more than that, one has to then choose to listen to that voice, cease hearing all the other possible voices in order to respond to that particular call. And here, we should perhaps attempt to not forget that the dossier of authority also brings with it the notion of authorship: and, more importantly, that the moment — or process, if you prefer — of authoring is the moment when the one who authors, brings something into being. For, the condition of authorship is that there is something that is being authored; and, more than that, that there is an « authority outside » oneself that recognises this act of authorship that has happened. And that, what is authored — even, and perhaps especially if it is the self — becomes, is brought forth as, is made into, *an object*.

Thus, it is only in her bondage to René — even to the extent that he is free to give her to Sir Stephen — that the love between them is written; to be more precise, authored. For O, « her freedom was worse than any chains. Her freedom was separating her from René ». One can — without much, if any, difficulty — detect a play on the Paulean notion of the Law here: not just that the Law writes its own transgression, which is why love should be the only Law, but that one should *love the very Law* itself. And it is only through fully embracing — in the precise sense of submission to — the law (in its Kafkaesque unknowability) that the possibility of freedom is potentially opened.

So, no longer a freedom as a relationality, a *freedom from*, but a *freedom in* the Law: where, at the point of entering the Law — stepping through the gate, as it were — the subject is now completely stripped of responsibility.

The trouble is: at the end of writing — at the point where one wants the writing to be sent out into the world — one has to name oneself as author; write, put, one's name down. And at the very moment of doing so, one also undoes one's authority — for, authority must be given to one. Why another gives it to one, why it is given to another, is another question entirely; one that perhaps has no answer. To compound matters, the moment one is authorised — perhaps through publishers, through a press, through a legal system that deems one the rightful author of a text — one is no longer able to read the text; one is separated from it. The text is emancipated from its author. Outside (ex-) *the grip of the ownership (mancipium); away from the grip* (manus; *hand) of the one who owns, the one who takes* (capere) *control*

[Which might be why O's thoughts only seem to ever appear within parenthesis. Which is not to say that what is parenthetical is less important: after all, as Derrida has taught us, the supplement is both an addition to and from within; more importantly, even as one may attempt to excise it, exorcise it even, it quite possibly remains to haunt the haunt.

Even if the haunt is precisely the Law itself.]

For, one should never forget that it in order for the Law to work — for it to have any power, perhaps even authority, over one — it has to first see one: even the infamous panoptical notion of self-governance, on disciplining the self, relies on one watching over one self, relies on sight.

Which also means that: the very condition of discipline is the self itself.
And perhaps this is the true radicality of O: freedom *over one. But once outside the law, one might well also be beyong the pale: for, one must never forget that if one is in language — at least in a manner that can be understood even if the understanding is provisional, momentary — one is always before the law. But once put before said law, language, and by extension, the text is also no longer one's own: it, and one — and one's relationality with the text, the law — is always already preceded by norms, mores, boundaries. Perhaps then, the only way to slip past the law, go by the gatekeeper, is to remain nameless: after all, the law can only be enacted on one it can name, call before itself.*

— Jeremy Fernando

through the undoing of her very self.

By disappearing.

Or, more precisely: by seeming to disappear. By — as Jean Baudrillard might say — *seducing with her very disappearance.*

By becoming, a *sex object.*

And as Baudrillard reminds us, « we must again praise the sex object; for it bears, in the sophistication of appearances, something of a challenge to the naïve order of the world and sex; and it alone, escapes the realm of production (though one might like to believe it subjected to the latter) and returns to that of seduction. In its unreality, in the unreal defiance of its prostitution of signs, the sexual object moves beyond sex and attains seduction. It again becomes ceremonial ».[16]

The great stars or seductresses never dazzle because of their talent or intelligence, but because of their absence.

— Jean Baudrillard

An enumeration of these practices would be interminable. But to confine ourselves to what our contemporaries vulgarly call 'the use of cosmetics', who can fail to see that the use of rice-powder (so stupidly anathematised by our candid philosophers) has the object and result of banishing from the complexion the blemishes which nature has so outrageously sown there, and of creating an abstract unity in the texture and colour of the skin; and that this unity, like the unity produced by the sculptor's chisel, brings the human being directly nearer to the statue …

— Charles Baudelaire

Where, it is not so much the a notion of erasure, or hiding — so commonly associated with cosmetics — that is important here, but rather that of a « banishing », where the possibility of « blemishes » no longer even remains in the same realm. Which opens the possibility that in the colloquial phrase *make-up*, the crucial term is not so much the *make* (even as *tekhnē* is with us, even as craft and skill are always already a condition of the possibility of sculpting), but the *up*, where cosmetics raises one to potentially being « nearer to the statue ». Of being not just « ceremonial » but celebrated, *revered.*

Where the ritual of putting on make-up, is precisely the ritual not so much of being offered, but of being sacrificed to. For, as Baudrillard continues, « artifice does not alienate the subject, but mysteriously alters her/him » by precisely making one « a pure appearance denuded of meaning ». And, more than that, « how can one mistake this 'exceeding of nature' for a vulgar camouflaging of truth?

Sacrifice destroys that which it consecrates. It does not have to destroy as fire does; only the tie that connected the offering to the world of profitable activity is severed, but this separation has the sense of a definitive consumption; the consecrated offering cannot be restored to the real order.

— Georges Bataille

Only falsehoods can alienate the truth, but makeup is not false, or else (like the game of transvestites) it is falser than false and so recovers a kind of superior innocence or transparency. It absorbs all expression within its own surface, without a trace of blood or meaning. Certainly this is challenging, and cruel — but who is alienated? Only those who cannot abide this cruel perfection, and cannot defend themselves except by moral repulsion — and they are wrong. How can one respond to pure appearances, whether hieratic or mobile, without first recognizing their sovereignty? By taking off the makeup, tearing off the veil, or enjoining the appearances to disappear? How ridiculous! An iconoclast's utopia. There is no God behind the images, and the very nothingness they conceal must remain a secret. The seduction, fascination and 'aesthetic' attraction of all the great imaginary processes lies here: in the effacing of every instance, be it the face and every substance, be it desire — in the artificial perfection of the sign ».[17]

Keeping in mind that mysteries can cause us to tremble — particularly if it is a mystery with nothing behind it, and thus, one that is completely and utterly unsolvable …

… *mysterium tremendum*

Which might be precisely why O commits herself to, one could even say propels herself towards, death — if not physically, at least not necessarily so, then certainly to the death of her self. Perhaps, she has learnt the lesson of the Nazarene. Not so much that — as Tim Rice might say — « to conquer death, you only have to die » — but, more radically, that *to disappear, you only have to die.* And, even as one might posit that *you only die twice* — once bodily, the other time when you are forgotten — the fact that no one has control over what they forget, alongside the lack of an object in forgetting, means that even as one has bodily been erased, one quite possibly remains to haunt the other, all others, by being part of their memories, even when they do not know it. For, « behind the only existing form of immortality, that of artifice, there lies the idea incarnated in the stars, that *death shines by its absence*, that death can be turned into a brilliant and superficial appearance, that it is itself a seductive surface … »[18]

… precisely by being *anything you want it to be.*

For what one, what we, should bear in mind is: even as O says that « no pleasure, no joy, no figment of her imagination could ever compete with the happiness she felt at the way he used her with such utter freedom, at the notion that he could do anything with her », even when she rejoices at the « delight and comfort, this iron ring which pierces the flesh and weighs one down forever, this mark eternal, how peaceful and reassuring the hand of a master who lays you on a bed of rock, the love of a master who know how to take what he loves ruthlessly, without pity »,[20] all of this is only possible because she wants it, she has agreed to it, has said *yes.*

That it is only « yes » which *begins us.*

That O only has given up her freedom because *she has.*

... most things, alas, have meaning and depth; but only some of them rise to the level of appearances, and they alone are truly seductive.

— Jean Baudrillard

comme O

Which brings us back to the very beginning of this chapter — to the mysterious quotation without a source, lines only known to one as the epigraph to *Histoire d'O;* and also in a section entitled 'Strange love letter' in Jean Paulhan's introduction, within which are lines that do not appear in the tale appear as well. Here, one could quite easily posit that Paulhan may have had access to earlier versions — after all, it is now widely known that Anna Desclos and him were lovers — or that he was reading a version that we are not privy to.

But that would be too easy; and, to be honest, rather uninteresting.

What strikes me — and here, I take responsibility for quite possibly mis-reading the text —, what stands out to me, is the title of the section: after all, one can never be sure where, if, or how, a letter lands: therefore, there is no reason to believe that *Histoire d'O*, if it is read as a missive, should affect us all in the same way. To Paulhan, it is « without doubt, *Story of O*, is the most ardent love letter any man has ever received ». And if written for him, there is not only no reason that we should be able to see all of it, but that even if one had read every single word that Paulhan did, one might still not be able to read it as he does.

After all, in his own words, « but to whom is the letter addressed? Whom is the speech trying to convince? Whom can we ask? I don't even know who you are ». Once again, perhaps performative: for the anonymity of the writer, the fact that Réage is a *nom de plume* adds to the allure — and marketing potential — of the book. But, perhaps also — at the very same time — a constative statement: for, even as Paulhan knows Desclos, even as they are lovers, there is no reason to believe he can ever know *who* she is.

Where, all Paulhan can do is to read *Histoire d'O* through another tale — through an account of a revolt in Barbados in 1838 where former slaves who, turned down by their previous master when attempting to convince him to « take them back under bondage »,[24] turned on him and massacred him and his entire family — whilst speculating that the « slaves were in love with their master ».[25] For, in his estimation « love implies dependence — not only in its pleasure but by its very existence and in what precedes its existence: in our very desire to exist — dependence on half a hundred odd little things: on two lips (and the smile or grimace they make), on a shoulder (and a special way it has of rising or falling), on two eyes (and their expression, a little more flirtatious or foreboding), or, when you come down to it, on the whole foreign body, with the mind and soul enclosed therein — a copy which is capable at any moment of becoming more dazzling than the sun, more freezing than a tract of snowy waste ».[26] Where perhaps in encountering — and it is quite possibly an event — the « foreign » body — both the text and Desclos — the stranger, *xenos*, that might be called the text of Pauline Réage, Paulhan can only open himself — be the host, attempt to be hospitable — to it, to its multiplicity, its unknowability. Where perhaps all he could do is to read an unknowable text through another instance of mystery, of secrecy: after all, one should try not to forget that the « notebook of grievances » around which the entire episode in Barbados hinges, « has never been recovered ».[27]

Where 'Strange love letter' is tautological — a triple repetition of, if not exactly the same, similar notions. Or, even: where 'strange love letter' is a triptych.

Just like how the « final chapter » of O's story « has been suppressed ». This, however, does not stop there being a « second ending to the story of O, according to which O, seeing that Sir Stephen was about to leave her, said she would prefer to die. Sir Stephen gave her his consent ». Which means that — like Jean Paulhan — all we can say is « I don't even know who you are ».

Where there remains a gap between the reader and the tale — whether the reader is one of *les immortels* or one of us who belong to the order of the dying is perhaps irrelevant —, where there remains a gap between one and another, any other, and where perhaps O is the name for nothing other than that gap.

Where O is quite possibly nothing other than one of the names of love.

***

… Ils se
regardent,
dans l'amour
le plus grand.
Amour sans
emploi, égorge
comme celui
de NEVERS.
Donc relégué
déjà dans
l'oubli. Donc
perpétuel.
(Sauvegardé
par l'oubli
même.) …

— Marguerite Duras

Really the
only reason I
write is so as
not to have
to deal with
myself!

— Elfriede Jelinek

Notes

On Fidelity

1 This particular notion of, relationality with, potentiality was opened to me in a conversation with Werner Hamacher.

2 The need for space in relation to touch was explored by Nancy — particularly in relation to love, relationality, closeness, and the possibility of rupturing, wounding, ripping when space is effaced — during his seminar, entitled *Art, Community, & Freedom*, at the European Graduate School, June, 2006.

3 Hanif Kureishi. *Intimacy*. London: Faber & Faber, 1999: 3.

4 Giorgio Agamben. *The Church and the Kingdom*, translated by Leland de la Durantaye. Calcutta: Seagull Books, 2012: 12.

5 *Aletheia*: 'truth, truthfulness',
from *alethes* 'true', literally 'not concealing', which is a combination of *a-* 'not' & *lethe* 'forgetfulness, oblivion'.
Lethe: one of the five river of Hades (whose water when drunk caused forgetfulness of the past), from the Greek *lethe*, literally 'forgetfulness, oblivion', which is related to *lethargos*, 'forgetful', and *lathre*, 'secretly, by stealth', *lathrios*, 'stealthy', *lanthanein*, 'to be hidden'.

6 *Ibid*: 9.

7 *Ibid*: 8.

8 And when one opens the dossier of attempts, of attempting, it also brings with it echoes of *tempting*, and *temptations*. Keeping in mind that to attempt first requires trying out (*temptare*), finding out: a sentiment that is not too difficult to hear in the primordial question in the garden, the question posed to the woman, the question of « did God really say you were not to eat from any of the tress in the garden? » (*Genesis* 3:1)

9 Alain Badiou with Nicholas Truong. *In Praise of Love*, translated by Peter Bush. London: Serpent's Tail, 2012: 29.

10 *Ibid*: 28.

11 *Ibid*: 33.

12 *Ibid*: 43.

13 Hanif Kureishi. *Intimacy*, 136.

14 Unfortunately, Kureishi fails to learn the lesson that he posits. For, the novel goes on one paragraph too long. By ending *Intimacy* with the protagonist and Nina getting back together and walking off into the sunset, it ends on a note that is too secure, too sure. And in that gesture, Kureishi undoes his very meditation on intimacy, and love; one that was captured perfect, so fleetingly, only lines before. At the point where the protagonist learns from his friend that Nina had called, and after picking up the phone, he changes his mind, replacing the receiver whilst musing, « Later … there will be time » (155). In bringing them together, Kureishi moves *intimacy* from a possibility — from something that requires movement;

metaphor — to the literal. And, in doing so, collapses the very gap that he posits is required for intimacy itself.

15 Alain Badiou with Nicholas Truong. *In Praise of Love*, 44.

16 *Ibid*: 85.

17 Werner Hamacher. 'The Promise of Interpretation: Remarks on the Hermeneutic Imperative in Kant and Nietzsche' in *Premises: Essays in Philosophy and Literature from Kant to Celan*, translated by Peter Fenves, Stanford: Stanford University Press, 1996: 142.

18 *Ibid: 133.*

19 *Ibid*: 133.

20 Herman Melville. *Bartleby the Scrivener: a story of Wall Street*. New Jersey: Melville Publishing House, 2008: 19.

21 *Ibid*: 25.

22 *Ibid*: 20.

23 *Ibid*: 18.

24 *Ibid*: 19.

25 *Ibid*: 19.

26 *Ibid*: 45.

27 *Ibid*: 42.

28 Avital Ronell. *Loser Sons: Politics & Authority*. Illinois: University of Illinois Press, 2012.

29 Herman Melville. *Bartleby the Scrivener*, 20.

30 *Ibid*: 41-44.

31 François Bizot. *The Gate*, translated by Euan Cameron. London: The Harvill Press, 2003: 119.

32 Avital Ronell. *Stupidity*. Chicago: University of Illinois Press, 2003: 73.
She continues: « … (Brecht, as you might recall, said that while intelligence is finite, stupidity is infinite; Einstein added: 'Two things are infinite: the universe and human stupidity, but I am not so certain about the universe.') ». [Quoted in Jerry Mayer & John P. Holmes (Eds). *Bite-sized Einstein*. New York: St. Martin's Press, 1996: 38.]

33 Umberto Eco. 'Interview: The Art of Fiction. No. 197' in *The Paris Review* (Summer 2008, No. 185).

34 Heraclitus. *Fragments*, translated by Brooks Haxton. London: Penguin Books, 2001.

And here, it is worth pausing to take note that Heraclitus is writing in fragments, in a fragmentary manner: but not just in relation with a text that is a missing whole, but also as a whole that is the fragment itself; as a reminder that as we read, that all reading itself, is always already a fragment. For, all we can do is attend to a part of a text, a fragment apart from the text as such — but in that moment of attention, the part is also our whole, occupies our entire being. Where « 112 » is a particular number in a sequence — one in a group of other numbers; but also, a singular entity onto itself — never forgetting that the sequential order is held together by the *zero*, a non-number, the *cipher*, the *secret*.

35 Miguel Cervantes. *Don Quixote*, translated by Walter Starkie. New York: Signet Classic, 2001:Volume 1, Chapter XXV, 247.

36 This would be consistent with his version of the world — attacking windmills as giants, challenging other non-existent 'knights', declaring himself a knight whilst forgetting that he is Alonso Quixana.

37 Avital Ronell. *Crack Wars: Literature, Addiction, Mania.* Lincoln: University of Nebraska Press, 1992.

38 Wallace Stevens. 'The Nobel Rider & the Sound of Words' in *The Necessary Angel: Essays on Reality & the Imagination.* New York: Vintage Books, 1965: 3-36.

39 Here, one might even posit that there is no difference between *I forget* and *I forgot.* For, since there is no object to forgetting, there is no way of discerning, differentiating, the aspect of *time*: and thus, both are always already present, past, and future — at the same time.

40 Georges Bataille. *On Nietzsche*, translated by Bruce Boon. London: continuum, 2004:19

41 Herman Melville. *Bartleby the Scrivener*, 50.

42 *Ibid*: 54.

43 *Ibid*: 43.

44 *Ibid*: 50.

45 *Ibid*: 47.

46 *Ibid*: 47.

47 Hélène Cixous. 'What is it o'clock? or The Door (we never enter)', translated by Catherine A.F. MacGillivray in *Stigmata*. New York: Routledge, 2005: 106.

48 Roland Barthes. *A Lover's Discourse: Fragments*, translated by Richard Howard. London: Vintage, 2002: 150-151.

49 *Ibid:* 150.

50 Giorgio Agamben. *The Church and the Kingdom*, translated by Leland de la Durantaye. London: Seagull Books, 2012: 4-5.

51 *Ibid*: 4.

52 *Ibid*: 9.

53 *Ibid*: 12.

54 *Ibid*: 26.

55 This is, perhaps, Samuel Beckett's lesson from *Waiting for Godot*: Vladimir and Estragon are waiting for nothing other than a name. For, even as they know that Godot exists — after all, at the end of each day, a little boy comes to tell them that Mr Godot will not be able to make it that day, but that he will the next — they do not know exactly who he is. Thus,

even if he had arrived — without referentiality to the name — they would not know if he were Godot or not. Which means that all Vladimir and Estragon can do is to either leave or wait: they would either cut all ties with the name, or continue waiting for Godot. Where all Vladimir and Estragon can do is to be in the moment of awaiting Godot, *en attendant Godot*. Where Godot is nothing but the name for waiting itself.

56 Roland Barthes. *A Lover's Discourse: Fragments*, 39.

57 This particular phrase was brought to my attention by Christian Baier, during a conversation with Dustin Hellberg and myself in Phuket, January, 2014.

Call me ...

1 Saint Augustine. *Confessions*, translated by Gary Wills. London: Penguin Classics, 2006: 3.

2 Jacques Derrida. *The Post Card: From Socrates to Freud and Beyond*, translated by Alan Bass. Illinois: University of Chicago Press, 1987: footnote, 21.

i, who weakened ...

1 *Judges* 16: 17

2 Søren Kierkegaard. *The Seducer's Diary*, translated by Howard V. Hong & Edna H. Hong, with a foreword by John Updike. Princeton: Princeton University Press, 1997: 146.

3 *Judges* 13: 20.

4 *Judges* 13: 19.

5 *Judges* 16: 28.

6 *Judges* 16: 20.

7 *Judges* 16: 30.

8 *Judges* 16: 31.

9 Hélène Cixous. *The Writing Notebooks of Hélène Cixous*, edited & translated by Susan Sellers. London: continuum, 2004: 29.

10 *Judges* 16: 25.

11 *Judges* 16: 20.

12 Jacques Derrida. *Glas*, translated by John P. Leavey Jr. & Richard Rand. Lincoln: University of Nebraska Press, 1990: 168.

Ce N'est Pas Un Calmar

1 « One morning, as the desire to take a walk came over me, I put on my hat, left my writing room, or room of phantoms, and ran down the stairs to hurry out into the street ».

Robert Walser. *The Walk*, translated by Christopher Middleton with Susan Bernofsky. New York: New Directions Books, 2012: 13.

2 Martin Heidegger. *What is Called Thinking?*, translated by J. Glenn Gray. New York: Perennial, 2004: 15.

3 For a more sustained meditation on reading as openness to nothing but the possibility of reading, please see my *Reading Blindly*. New York: Cambria Press, 2010.

4 Alain Badiou with Nicolas Truong. *In Praise of Love*, translated by Peter Bush. London: Serpent's Tail, 2012: 16.

5 « All this », so I proposed resolutely, « I shall soon sketch and write down in a piece or sort of fantasy, which I shall entitle 'The Walk' ».

Robert Walser. *The Walk*, 32

6 Maurice Blanchot. *The Step Not Beyond*, translated by Lycette Nelson. Albany: State University of New York Press, 1992: 34.

7 *Ibid*: 35.

8 *Ibid*: 39.

9 Maurice Blanchot. *The Step Not Beyond*, 116.

10 Avital Ronell. *Dictations: On Haunted Writing*. Lincoln: University of Nebraska Press, 1993.

11 Michel Foucault. *Speech Begins after Death: In conversation with Claude Bonnefoy*, edited by Philippe Artières & translated by Robert Bononno. Minnesota: University of Minnesota Press, 2013: 44.

12 « *quand, j'interroge Eve est-ce pour lui donner laparole, ou pour la lui prendre?* »
Hélène Cixous. *The Writing Notebooks of Hélène Cixous*, edited and translated by Susan Sellers. London: continuum, 2004: 37.

13 Michel Foucault. *Speech Begins after Death: In conversation with Claude Bonnefoy*, 79-80.

14 *Ibid:* 80-81.

15 *Ibid*: 79.

16 *Ibid*: 38.

17 *Ibid*: 46.

18 *Ibid*: 45.

19 *Ibid*: 44.

20 *Ibid*: 38.

21 Robert Walser. *The Walk*, 38.

22 Hélène Cixous. *Les réveries de la femme sauvage: scènes primitives*. Paris: Editions Galilée, 2000: 9-10, translated by Susan Sellers in *The Writing Notebooks of Hélène Cixous*. London: continuum, 2004: vii.

Love Letters

1 A phrase that was uttered to me during a conversation — which touched on, amongst many other things, Kraus' line on love letters — during the evening of 11 November, 2013.

2 Roland Barthes. *A Lover's Discourse: Fragments*, translated by Richard Howard. London: Vintage Classics, 2002: 73.

3 This is a notion that Derrida continually explores throughout his work, his thought, in

particular when attempting to think about the relationality between love (*l'amour*) and death (*la mort*).

4 Perhaps the only appropriate, apt, space, to place the notes to a love song is in an endnote; hidden away from prying eyes, where it can attempt to slip past appropriation, seizing, grasping, apprehension, comprehension. Perhaps then, it is always also a silent love song, a long song of silence — or, even silence as a love song. But, always already, for her.

5 Jean Genet. 'The strange word *Urb*' in *Reflections on the Theatre and Other Writings*, translated by Richard Seaver. London: Faber & Faber, 2009: 70.

6 Jacques Derrida. *Glas*, translated by John P. Leavey Jr. & Richard Rand. Lincoln: University of Nebraska Press, 1990: 82.

7 *Ibid*: 82.

8 Elfriede Jelinek. *Her Not All Her: on/with Robert Walser*, translated by Damion Searls. Paris: Slyph Editions, 2012: 7.

9 *Ibid*: 5.

10 *Ibid*: 5.

11 *Ibid*: 27.

Objectify me please ...

1 Søren Kierkegaard. *The Seducer's Diary*, translated by Howard V. Hong & Edna H. Hong, with a foreword by John Updike. Princeton: Princeton University Press, 1997: 146.

2 Marilyn Manson. 'Devour' in *The High End of Low*. (California: Interscope, 2009).

3 All quotes from Heinrich Kleist's 'On the Marionette Theatre' are from Idris Parry's 1978 translation for the *London Times Literary Supplement*, which is available at http://www.southerncrossreview.org/9/kleist.htm

4 'The slow-burning Polanski saga' in *BBC News* (28 September, 2009): http://news.bbc.co.uk/2/hi/entertainment/8278256.stm

5 Jacques Rancière. *The Aesthetic Unconscious*, translated by Debra Keates & James Swenson. London: Polity Press, 2009: 24.

6 *Ibid*: 6.

7 *Ibid*: 24.

8 *Ibid*: 24.

9 Geraldine Song. *Absence—Presence*. Singapore: Metonymy Press, 2014.

10 '—' in *Ibid*: 34.

11 Barry Gibb & Robin Gibb. 'To Love Somebody' in *Bee Gees 1st*. London: Polydor Records, 1967.

12 Werner Hamacher. 'Interventions'. in *Qui Parle: Journal of Literary Studies* 1, no. 2, Spring 1987: 37-42.

13 Pauline Réage. *Story of O: a novel*, translated by Sabine d'Estrée. New York: Ballantine Books, 2013: 91.

14 *Ibid*: 123.

15 *Ibid*: 99.

16 Jean Baudrillard. *Seduction*, translated by Brian Singer. New York: St. Martin's Press, 1990: 92.

17 *Ibid*: 94.

18 *Ibid*: 97.

19 Pauline Rèage. *Story of O*, 185.

20 *Ibid*: 180.

21 Jean Paulhan. 'Happiness in Slavery' in *The Story of O*, xxix.
Here, it is also possible to open the question of whether Paulhan was quoting from the text, or whether the epigraph quotes Paulhan: a question that — since both parties involved are dead — might well remain unanswered. And, even if Desclos and Paulhan had responded to the question, there is no way of knowing, with any certainty, whether their answer had any relation with the question. One can find a echo of this uncertainty in the status of the so-called sequel, *Retour à Roissy*, which — whilst attributed to Réage — Desclos says she had naught to do with.

22 *Ibid*: xxxi.

23 *Ibid*: xxiv.

24 *Ibid*: xxi.

25 *Ibid*: xxxv.

26 *Ibid*: xxi.

27 *Ibid*: 196.

Jeremy Fernando is the Jean Baudrillard Fellow at the European Graduate School, where he is also a Reader in Contemporary Literature & Thought. He works in the intersections of literature, philosophy, and the media; and has written fifteen books — including *Reading Blindly*, *Living with Art*, and *Writing Death*. His work has been featured in magazines and journals such as *Berfrois*, *CTheory*, *TimeOut*, and *VICE*, amongst others; and he has been translated into Japanese, Italian, Spanish, and Slovenian. Exploring other media has led him to film, music, and art; and his work has been exhibited in Seoul, Vienna, Hong Kong, and Singapore. He is the editor of the thematic magazine *One Imperative*; and is a Fellow of Tembusu College at the National University of Singapore.

www.ingramcontent.com/pod-product-compliance
Lightning Source LLC
Chambersburg PA
CBHW040016240426
43664CB00037B/37